The Knitting Bible 2023

5 in 1

The Ultimate Collection of Easy-to-Follow
Patterns from Beginners to Advanced

Martha Wayne

TABLE OF CONTENTS

INTRODUCTION

Fundamentals of Knitting

What is Knitting?

Knitting is creating fabric with yarn and two or more needles. Loops are formed on one needle as a starting point, and the fabric grows gradually by drawing other loops through them as they are passed back and forth on the needles, row by row.

Knitting is the process of making cloth out of yarn or thread. Knitted fabrics are made up of stitches, rows of loops connected in a row. A new loop is drawn through an old loop as each row advances. A needle holds the active stitches until another loop can be threaded through them. The entire process will result in a fabric that can be utilized to create clothing.

Knitting can be dòne with a machine or by hand. However, in this book, we'll look at how to knit with your own hands. When you do it that way, it gives you a lot of satisfaction and enjoyment. Hand knitting encompasses a wide range of styles and methods.

Various needles and yarns are used to create the knitted material, which can vary in texture, color, integrity, and weight. The person doing the knitting is the most crucial factor.

To begin your knitting journey, understand the difference between right and left-hand needles and how to hold the needles and yarns.

Beginning knitters may become overwhelmed by the variety of available yarns, needles, and patterns. But if you stick with it, you'll soon discover that knitting is very simple, and you only need to learn two stitches to make any knitted item: the knit and purl stitches. So, are you ready to join the party?

In today's world, where everyone is rushing to reach their goals and destinations, nurturing a hobby such as knitting may seem out of place. Nobody has time to sit back and visit with those they care about. Why should we do that when we can just pick up our cell phones? Everything is at our fingertips, whether keeping in touch or sending them gifts.

Knitting has an appeal, as many people who are already enamored with and knowledgeable about this hobby have discovered. You may have already become well-known among friends or family for your exceptional knitting skills. When others are envious of your new knitted and stylish scarves, gloves, or shrugs, those envious facial expressions will encourage you to hone your talent.

Our goal with this book is to assist those who are already in love with knitting but don't know where to start. Although an unlimited wealth of information is available on the internet, finding a clean and risk-free way to get started always appears difficult for beginners. Keeping this in mind, this book has been designed to provide the greatest benefit to the beginner, particularly those unfamiliar with the term "knitting." I believe that by the end of the journey, you will realize that knitting is not as complex as it appears.

Unlike other hobbies such as gardening or reading, knitting is less time-consuming and even helps to enhance multitasking capability. Usually, those who indulge in knitting rarely suffer from a bad mood or depression and eventually find themselves happier than others.

Knitting plays a vital role in keeping our brains active. While you are struggling with those complicated stitches or trying to secure dropped stitches, you are helping your brain work more, enhancing its working capabilities. This beautiful skill allows room for experimenting with different types of stitches, which means there will never be a shortage of creative ideas and projects. You are undoubtedly on the right track if you choose knitting as your favorite hobby to be passionate about.

For elderly people, knitting is a beautiful pastime, especially when they have no one to give them company and are retired and unable to get out of the house much. Experimenting with those complicated stitches does not allow them time to feel lonely. If they are beginners, joining a knitting class can significantly help them. They can make friends along with learning knitting. Younger generations are also on the list of admirers, particularly when they want to show off their talents. Knitting as a hobby allows their talents to flourish and keeps them away from wrongdoings by giving them something meaningful to take up their time. They remain relaxed and stress-free.

The Right and Left Hand Needle Comparison

- Right-Hand Needle: As if you were holding a pencil, hold the right-hand needle. Pass the knitted piece over the hand between the thumb and the index finger when casting on and working the first few rows. Grasping the needle from below, let your thumb slide under the knitted piece as your work progresses.

- Left-Hand Needle: Using the thumb and index finger, hold the left needle lightly over its top to control the needle's tip.

How to Hold the Needles and the Yarn

In holding knitting needles and yarn, many people have evolved or upgraded their way of doing it. However, it's still best and useful to know how to start.

- 1st Method. While holding the yarn through your right hand, let the yarn go under the small finger, go around the same finger, let it hover over the third finger, go under your third finger (the middle one), and lastly, over the index finger. Your index finger must pass the yarn around the needle tip. One thing to remember: the yarn circling the little finger controls the tension on the yarn.

- 2nd Method. While holding the yarn through your right hand, let the yarn go under the small finger, through under your center finger, and above your index finger. You must use your index finger to let the yarn go through around the needle tip. In Method 2, remember that gripping the yarn in the crook of your little finger controls the tension.

There are two primary methods of handling your yarn when knitting, but both types can be done easily and yield the same results with practice.

Continental (or European) knitting is called keeping the working yarn in the left hand, which needs less hand movement. American (or English) knitting is called keeping it on the right.

Which one do you pick? Mostly, the distinction is a personal choice. As it requires less hand movement and thus less repeated stress on the joints, I typically teach Continental first. Try American if you find it challenging to keep your stress right or master the necessary movements. You may also find reasons to use both on the same project as you become more experienced (as in when working with two colors in stranded knitting).

American style is often called "throwing" in knitting lingo because of how you have to "throw" the yarn around the needle to make a new stitch, and Continental is called "picking" because you simply need to "pick" up with a tiny needle movement to catch the new yarn. The war of tossing vs. picking rages on is good fun because it's up to you, the knitter, to decide what's best for you.

Knitting is an ambidextrous activity, so right-handed and left-handed knitters can attempt both knitting types to see which is simpler.

The first important thing to learn when you knit is how to keep your working yarn under good tension. It's easier to shape stitches by keeping good tension, and the resulting stitches are more even. Bad tension makes it hard to knit, is stressful, and leads to shoddy-looking results.

By constantly holding your working yarn taut, good tension is produced. One of the main causes of problematic stitch formation is this.

Your knitting style, or in which hand you carry your working yarn, will decide how you keep your yarn taut.

- Knitting "English" Style

The yarn in the right hand is kept up by American knitting. This is much less precise than Continental, as after it has been looped around the needle, the tension is created by pulling on the yarn with the right hand.

The right hand's fingers are wrapped in yarn. The goal is to control the yarn tightly but with a relaxed hand, releasing it as the stitches are shaped to flow through the fingers.

Try this alternative form, too, or make your own. To build even loops that are neither too loose nor too tight, you need to tense the yarn just enough with your fingers.

Keep the needles in your left hand and the other in your right hand with the stitches about to work. Wrap the thread around the needle with your right index finger.

- Knitting "Continental" Style

The yarn is kept in the left hand by continental knitting. You don't need to wrap your hand exactly the way I do, but it's necessary to maintain a firm tension on the working yarn while allowing it to slip smoothly over the hand, even though you wrap the yarn.

Lace the yarn in some way that feels relaxed through the fingers of your left hand. To create uniform loops, try to release and tense the yarn quickly.

The yarn is wound twice around your index finger in this alternate technique.

Keep in your left hand the needle with the unworked stitches and in your right hand the other needle. With your left index finger, place the yarn and pull it with the tip of the right needle through the loops.

How to Pick Your Yarn

Even advanced knitters get astonished by the selection of available yarn. There are just so many beautiful choices! There is always something new. You can fritter away days through the different options, enjoying the textures and the colors.

Choose a medium yarn weight rather than thin or thick. Make sure the texture is smooth. This will be the easiest to learn and practice on. When purchasing from a commercial yarn or craft store, always read the label wrapped around the ball for more important details about the yarn you are considering. You may find that some will indicate that it is better for certain crafts than others.

Reading a yarn label can be challenging for those who have never looked at one. Below are some tips on how to decipher the yarn label code:

- The Largest Letters: The company's names are the letters or words dominating the label.
- Net Weight: This indicates the bulk of the yarn: light, medium, or bulky. Look for the number "4" on the label. This indicates it is medium. "0" is for lace, "1" and "2" are fine, and "3" is light. "5" and "6" are bulky, and "7" indicates a jumbo weight.
- Length: This is the total amount of yarn you will get in a ball. Ensure that the length is equal to or more than the project you are planning. If it is not, you will need to pick up more balls.
- Color and Color Number: Typically, a name is given to the color. It can be generic like "Bright Red" or more creative like "Robin Red Breast." A more specific color number is associated with the color, like "A432." Suppose you purchase more than one ball of yarn for a project; double-check that the color and color name are the same. The color may appear similar, but when you mix the two balls, you notice subtle differences. It is best to do a little check here to avoid a disaster later.
- Dye Lot: Similar to checking the color name and number, this Dye Lot number indicates that the yarn was colored in the same batch. Again, this can slightly alter the color of the yarn even if they have the same color name and number. This will be listed as a simple combination of numbers like "567."
- Fiber Content: This number and name will be given together. It will appear as a single fiber and percentage, such as "100% wool," or a combination of fibers and percentages, such as "50% acrylic, 50% wool." When beginning many projects, stick to more natural fibers like wool and avoid acrylic because they will split and slip on your needles. Additionally, despite being a natural fiber, cotton has little flexibility and can be difficult for beginners to work with.
- Gauge and Laundry Symbols: Sometimes, the care instructions will only be given to you in words and images.
-

How to Pick Your Needles

You may notice that there are hundreds of different options for knitting needles. They come in all sorts of sizes and materials. Some people swear by bamboo or wood needles, while others love metal, such as aluminum ones. Others enjoy the variety and economic benefits of plastic needles. As you continue practicing and trying out different tools, you will develop a preference, like every knitter.

To begin, select a couple of different-sized needles to try out. Do not shy away from the curved, circular needles either. These may end up being your best friend. Circular needles allow you to knit flat and hold many more stitches than flat needles. This is especially handy for large projects. Many knitters love working with wooden needles, especially in the beginning, because of the strength and slight give in the material. They also grip the yarn well, unlike smooth options like some plastics and most metals.

As previously suggested, start with medium yarn and knit with medium-sized needles. Check for sizes like 6 US, 7 US, or 8 US. Choose 4 mm, 4.5 mm, or 5 mm if the needles do not have US sizes. These are best for medium yarns and feel good in your hands. This also applies to the thickness of the needle. Thin needles are great for thinner yarn, while thicker needles complement thick yarn better. If you have a medium-weight wool yarn, choose a needle with a medium thickness.

Another consideration is the needle length. This mainly applies to straight needles, but the needles range in size from 7 to 14 inches. Children typically use the smaller needles, but you may like the shorter sizes in the beginning. Shorter needles can be less difficult to maneuver and easier to use. If a project is large, choose a longer needle so it can hold more stitches.

Knitting Terms Glossary

Knitters have a language all their own. As you move beyond this book, you will encounter books and patterns that use a variety of standard abbreviations. Here's a list of what you need to know to understand the instructions.

- * : Repeat the instructions between the two asterisks.
- Alt: alternate (as in "alt rows").
- Beg: beginning
- Bet: between
- BO: bind off
- CA: color A (when you are using more than one color)
- CB: color B (see above)
- CC: contrasting color (ditto!)
- Cn: cable needle, which could be either a small hook or something that looks like an overgrown toothpick with a curve in the middle, used to hold stitches when making a cable stitch
- Cont: continue
- Dec: decrease
- DK: double knitting; a yarn weight or knitting technique
- Dp, dpn: double-pointed needle
- EON: end of the needle
- EOR: end of row
- Fl: front loop
- Foll: follow or following
- G st: garter stitch (knitting every row)
- Incl: including
- K: knit
- K tbl: knit through the back loop, which creates a twist on the finished stitch
- K1 f&b: knit into the front of the stitch and then into the back of the same stitch
- K2tog: knit two stitches together
- K2tog tbl: knit two stitches together through the back loop instead of the front
- LC: left cross, a cable stitch where the front of the cross slants to the left
- LH: left hand
- Lp: loop
- LT: left twist, a stitch that creates a mock cable slanted to the left
- M1: Make one stitch, which requires an increase method
- MC: main color
- P: purl

- P tbl: purl through the back loop instead of the front
- P up: pick up
- P2tog: purl two stitches together
- P2tog tbl: purl two stitches together through the back loop instead of the front
- Patt: pattern
- Pm: place stitch marker
- Prev: previous
- Psso: pass slipped stitch over (as in binding off)
- Pu: pick up (stitches)
- RC: right cross, a cable stitch where the front of the cross slants to the right
- Rem: remaining
- Rep: repeat
- RH: right hand
- Rnd: round(s); when knitting on a circular or double-pointed needle, when the yarn is joined, you knit in rounds, not rows
- RS: right side
- RT: right twist, a stitch that creates a mock cable slanted to the right
- Sk: skip
- Sk2p: slip one stitch, knit two together, and then pass the slipped stitch over the knitted ones to create a double decrease
- Skp: slip one stitch, knit one stitch, and then pass the slipped stitch over the knitted one to create a single decrease
- Sl, slst, slip: slip or slide a stitch without working it
- Sl, k1, psso: same as "skp"
- Sl1k: slip one stitch knit-wise
- Sl1p: slip 1 stitch purlwise
- Ssk: slip one stitch, slip the next stitch, and then knit the two stitches together to create a left-slanting decrease
- Ssp: slip one stitch, slip the next stitch, and then purl the two stitches together to create a right-slanting decrease
- Sssk: slip one stitch, slip the next stitch, slip the 3rd, and then knit the three stitches together to create a double, left-slanting decrease
- St: stitch
- Sts: stitches
- St st: stockinette stitch; alternately knit a row and purl a row

- Tbl: through the back loop (of a stitch)
- Tog: together
- WS: wrong side
- Wyib: with yarn in back
- Wyif: with yarn in front
- Yfwd: yarn forward (same as yarn over)
- Yo: yarn over, move yarn to the opposite direction
- Yrn: yarn 'round needle (same as yarn over)

Getting Started with Knitting

To start with, all you need is some yarn and some needles. To make the interlocking loops more visible, I chose medium-weight yarn and larger needles. The majority of knitting is done a little tighter than this.

- Step 1: There's a little theory involved.

It's essentially just a sequence of interlocking loops that make up knitting. Re-examine the photograph from the front. I used a yellow thread in one row to make it simpler to see how the loops interact.

There is no difference between a knit and a purl stitch, except that the purl is stitched from the other side. Interlocking V's are facing you while you're knitting, and interlocking U's are facing you when you're purling.

Starter loops are used to "cast on" a knitting needle and begin knitting. When it's the right size, you'll continue knitting until you reach that point. You'll "cast off" or shut off all the loops to prevent the knitting from unraveling again.

Additionally, various methods exist to hold the needles and yarn when knitting. There are other ways to do this, but I'm going to go with the Continental technique in this tutorial (pic 3). Alternatively, this end may be held in the right hand, which is more typical in the United States, but in my view, is less efficient.

- Step 2: Casting on

You may cast on in several different ways. Although it isn't the simplest, is adaptable and durable (which tends to unravel itself, causing dismay, grief, and dropped stitches).

For those who like to read rather than look at visuals, here are some options:

- Make a slip knot, leaving a tail roughly three times your item's finishing width. If you're right-handed, place the slip knot on the needle with your right hand (for lefties, you can try it this way or reverse it, whichever works for you). The long tail should be held in the left hand and cinched around the first finger, as in the illustration.
- Place your finger and needle in a loop by placing the needle's tip beneath your finger's loop (pics 2 & 3). Using your right hand, take a strand of yarn from the ball or skein and bring it over the finger loop, between your finger and the needle, to complete the stitch (pics 4, 5, & 6).
- Slip the right-hand yarn piece off your finger and across the needle's tip (pics 7, 8, & 9). Close the loop by gently tugging the left-hand yarn end, causing the right-hand yarn end to loop around the needle (pics 10 & 11).
- Since the initial slip knot counts as the first stitch, you now have two stitches on your needle.
- Repeat this process until you've made an adequate number of stitches. 12 or 16 swatches are plenty for a beginner's kit. Do you know how many I had by the time I was done?

- Step 3: Knitting

Knitting's fundamental stitches are divided into two categories depending on the direction in which the yarn is pulled through the loop. You can knit or purl, depending on whatever method you like. Stitches are stitched from the left needle to the right needle in both cases. Switch hands when the right needle is filled and the left is empty.

To knit, follow these steps:

- Your left hand must hold the yarn, as illustrated. Wrap the yarn tail around your fingers in a manner that feels natural; the idea is to keep it taut but not so tight that you can't take more out as required. Some people wrap it twice around their pinkie.
- The first or next loop on the left should be the right-hand needle's starting point (pic 1). Using your left forefinger, wrap the yarn counter-clockwise around the needle on the right hand (pic 2). Slipping the needle underneath the yarn is another way to describe this.

- Bring the yarn from the left hand back through the initial loop, keeping it wrapped around the needle (pics 3 and 4). It's far simpler to do it than it is to explain it.
- To finish, remove the old loop from the left needle while retaining a new loop on the right needle (pic 5). That's one knit stitch down!

- Step 4: Purling

In knitting, the purl stitch is the knit stitch reversed. Instead of working your way forward from the front, you'll work your way backward from the rear and draw a loop through the front.

Now, work the yarn in the opposite direction of the needle's rotation, or up and over the needle and to the left. Pull the yarn through the loop by catching it with the right needle's tip. Keeping the left needle tip pointing towards your body assists with this maneuver.

It is time to remove the old loop but maintain the one you inserted into it on the right needle. You've successfully finished a purl stitch!

- Step 5: Casting off

The knitting and purling are done; therefore, you're all done. What's the best way to come to a complete halt without letting any loops fall apart?

You may cast off by holding the work as if you were about to knit another row before releasing the yarn. Cast off one stitch by knitting (knitting is simpler than purling, but you can also cast off purl-wise). It's time to bring that stitch across to your right-hand needle. Instead of putting the right needle into the final stitch on the left, insert it into two stitches - the one you slid onto and the one directly in front of it. Pull the loop through the two stitches one at a time. So far, you've only knit one stitch on the right needle, but you've already created two.

This is the best way to cover the whole length. One stitch will remain after the pattern. Pull the cut end of your yarn through this loop to secure it, then tighten it.

- Step 6: Add to your resources

Here are a few key terms:

- Instead of purling, the Garter Stitch is used while knitting a row. This creates a ribbing with a lot of vertical strain in the transverse direction.
- Knit a row, turn, and purl the next row in stockinette stitch. On one side, it has all the knit-looking stitches, while on another, it has just purl-looking ones.
- Knits and purls are alternated vertically. Wrist, hem, and necklines are all common places to see this trim on sweaters. Until now, I didn't have an example of this to show you, but I can bet you do.

- In reality, dropping a stitch off the left-side needle without first pulling another loop through it is an error. This will produce a run, or ladder, which will unravel a row if you don't correct it.
- Decreasing: the most common instance of removing. When sewing a curved edge, such as a neckline, you may wish to utilize this technique when you don't want to complete all of the stitches.

Tools

Needles

The pattern will usually tell you what size of needles to use. Single-pointed straight needles are about 7 to 14 inches in length and come in sizes 000 to 16. They are made of aluminum, plastic, or wood and are used for regular, flat knitting. Circular needles aren't circular; they're just made up of two needle tips linked by a cable. These are used to knit items that are circular or items that are very wide.

The range can seem daunting when you pick out your first pair of knitting needles. A particular type of needle, straight, circular, or double-pointed, is probably needed by your pattern. It helps to know how to use each form if it doesn't, or even if it does, and when one can be substituted for another.

Experienced knitters, however, according to their knitting style and tension, frequently decide on a chosen needle type. Needles come in various kinds and are made of various materials, and using unique methods or dealing with certain fabrics has advantages. Find out here how to pick the most fitting needles you have in mind for the project.

Straight Needles

This needle is pointed at one end with a stop on the other or a guard. It is used for knitting "flat" or back and forth. Most beginner patterns use this type of needle.

When knitting, straight needles provide a great deal of help to the hand. These are what you should start with if you are new to knitting. For small projects, short needles are recommended; long needles are more suitable for larger knits, such as a pullover or blanket for an infant, and for knitters who prefer to work by keeping the needles under their arms or elbows.

Circular Needles

This needle has two pointed ends, linked by a flexible cord, at the required needle size. The cables have different lengths. For flat or circular knitting, circular needles may be used (not to be confused with cable needles, though they have a cable). You would only knit from one side to the other if you were knitting in a circle; no turning was required.

In this situation, choose a cable length roughly the same or slightly shorter than your project's diameter. If your cable is too long, that's all right. You can still use it by cutting out the excess cable length between stitches in a loop. However, you will constantly have to do so when you work around your project.

Some knitted flat projects are too wide and bulky for straight needles that are typically no longer than 14 inches/35 cm. (Think of Afghans, big cardigans knitted in one piece, etc.) You can use circular needles in that situation. At least 40'/100 cm, pick a very long cable and handle the two ends like straight needles. Work the first row, for example, then transform the job as you would for straight needles and work back your way.

Double-Pointed Needles

On both ends, these needles have points and range in length from 4"/10 cm to 9"/22.5 cm. They are used in the round for knitting and come in sets of at least four, three to keep the stitches and one to work the next stitches on.

For very small projects, double-pointed needles (dpns) may also be used as flat needles shorter than the needle length (such as a gauge swatch.)

Cable Needles

This needle with a bend in it can be shaped like a hook or a double-pointed needle. When producing cables and texture stitches, it is used to keep stitches away from the main work. Your pattern should say so if you need this form of a needle.

Needle Materials

Plastic, wood, bamboo, or metal may be made of needles. Each material feels different to work with, "grabs" yarn differently, and, when you work, creates varying amounts of noise. The needle you use will depend more on availability and personal preference.

For most projects, since they are quieter and have a little more friction than metal, I prefer wood or bamboo needles (so the stitches don't fall off when I don't want them to), and they feel better than plastic, plus, they're not as easily bent. I do not suggest metal needles for beginners, as stitches appear to fall very quickly off them.

Metal Needles

Slippery metal needles are perfect for hairy fabrics such as mohair or wool, which can stick. The slippery surface will help if you find that you prefer to knit too tightly because it will allow the tension of a knitter to loosen. Needles with a diameter of more than US11 (UK0/8mm) can be clunky to deal with, so they are seldom used.

Ebony/Rosewood Needles

To work with, these wooden needles feel luxurious and can be very costly. They also have a waxy surface, which, with wear, becomes smooth, producing a soft and touchy surface. They help to build an even tension, like bamboo needles; they maintain their shape and stay straight when used, giving them a strong feeling.

Plastic Needles

Choose plastic for needles with a surface halfway between metal and that bamboo. During use, plastic stays at a steady temperature, which may suit individuals who have arthritis. Avoid US6 (UK8/4mm) plastic needles or smaller ones, as heavy projects can bend or break them.

Bamboo Needles

Bamboo is a lightweight, durable fiber and makes excellent needles for knitting. It helps to keep stitches regularly spaced, making a fabric with good tension that is evenly knitted. Good for fibers like silk, mercerized cotton, and slippery bamboo yarn. Recommended for people living with arthritis. Thin needles, to accommodate the curvature of your palm, can gradually warp slightly with use.

Square Needles

With a pointed tip, most needles are cylindrical; these rare new needles have a faceted surface and a pointed tip. Made of metal, they lay best on each other, which is especially useful when dealing with double-pointed needles, creating less pressure on the hands and making them particularly good for patients with arthritis.

Tapestry Needles

These have a blunt tip to prevent fiber damage, making them ideal for use by knitters. Ensure that the eye is sufficient for the yarn: do not push or spoil the yarn into an eye that is too small.

Tips or Corks

Tips or corks can protect your fingertips from the strong and sharp points of the knitting needles. In addition, these prevent stitches from sliding off the needles.

Measuring Tools

A good measuring tape, a ruler, or a measuring tape should always be handy to measure your progress.

Scissors

For obvious reasons, a good pair of scissors should always be present.

Tapestry Needle

A dull-pointed tapestry needle is used for sewing the seams of your garment.

Knit Check

A knit check is a helpful tool to measure the number of stitches and rows you have made per square inch. The holes on the top are used to measure the needle size.

Yarn

Yarn is the long spun, stranded fiber we use to knit. There are several kinds of yarn, enabling knitters to appreciate as they express themselves through the medium of a range of sensory experiences. The yarn can be made of various fibers and has a variety of textures.

The possibilities are exciting: from a skein of flexible silk sock yarn to the plastic bag you used to carry it home, you can knit with everything. Choose from a color palette that varies from subtle, subdued tones to bright ones that pop into the eyes.

Fibers

Yarns are made from fibers, as are fabrics. Fiber can be an animal's fur, manmade (synthetic), or plant-derived. To produce yarn, the fibers are processed and spun. To boost its characteristics, yarn can be made from a single fiber, such as wool, or blended with other fibers (for example, to affect its durability or softness). Numerous blends are frequently created for aesthetic reasons, such as adding a lustrous sheen by combining wool and expensive silk. All yarns have unique qualities. As a result, making it essential to select the right blend for your project.

Natural Fibers

- Wool

The wool fleece is made into pure wool yarns of several sheep breeds, such as the Shetland and Blue-faced Leicester, or mixed with other fibers. It is warm, waterproof, and great for wearing coats, cardigans, caps, and gloves in winter. Rough-feeling wool has short, coarse fibers that irritate, so it is safer to knit garments worn next to the skin with softer forms. Unless "super wash" is labeled, wool should always be hand-washed carefully.

- Merino Wool

This unique wool is from the sheep merino, which has one of the finest wools of any breed of sheep. The long, lustrous fibers create a soft yarn that is a perfect choice for products like scarves, arm warmers, and children's clothing that will be worn against the skin. It is typically combined with other fibers and is also handled to make it washable by machine.

- Mohair

It is a fiber made from the hair of the angora goat. When knitted up, it creates a special natural "halo." It is very hard to work with it because its blurred nature makes it difficult to see the knitting structure and any errors made. Mohair makes oversized sweaters and accessories that are particularly fascinating. It is not recommended for making baby clothing, as when freshly made, it can shed hair, which could be hazardous if inhaled.

- Alpaca

This fiber is one of the warmest natural fibers you can use for knitting and has a luxurious feel. Even a fine, sport-weight garment offers ample insulation in bitterly cold weather. The alpaca is llama related. Alpaca yarn is excellent for ski hats and thick, comfortable sweaters and socks. You can also find usable baby alpaca yarn that is even softer.

- Cashmere

This fiber is a soft goat's undercoat that provides an ultra-luxurious, velvety-soft yarn. It is light but solid and typically offers more yardage per gram in other fibers than comparable yarns. Cashmere is a costly fiber to manufacture and is often mixed with other fibers to add softness and a touch of luxury. It should be enjoyed in scarves, cowls, or sweaters close to the skin. This fiber is only ever hand-washed.

- Angora

A soft and long fiber is produced by the lush coat of the angora rabbit. It is similar to mohair. Yarns that have a furry "halo" effect are mixed with other fibers to create them. Each hair is very silky, and although soft, the resulting spun yarns appear to shed fibers. Angora makes delightful knits, but it is very delicate, so bags or housewares are not recommended. Check the ball band for treatment guidance, as with other fragile fibers.

- Matte Cotton

The fluffy mass that forms around the seeds of the cotton plant is cotton. It gets spun into a summery, breathable fiber. Various cotton yarns are easy to wash and can be extremely durable, and last for decades when properly cared for. Therefore, it is a fine fiber for housewares, knitted pouches, and shoulder bags. For hand-dyeing, pure, untreated cotton is ideal.

- Mercerized Cotton

It is possible to mercerize cotton yarn, a procedure during which mechanical and chemical processing is done to compact it, making it into an ultra-strong yarn with a reflective sheen that does not shed lint. Mercerized cotton is typically a more costly alternative. Still, it is suitable for a project that needs to be strong and retain its shape, such as a polished evening purse, a long summer cardigan, or a frequently washed throw.

- Silk

The silkworm is a caterpillar that eats the leaves of mulberry and spins a cocoon in which it becomes a moth. The caterpillar extrudes a fine silk filament to make the cocoon; these filaments are twisted together to create silk thread. The silk of the mulberry is very fine, lustrous, and smooth, while the silk moth of the tussah is slightly thicker and less lustrous; both are very solid. Silk fiber has always been costly due to its particular source. Its luxurious texture makes it perfect for wedding and christening gifts and indulgent, tailored knitwear.

- Linen

The flax plant is usually produced from this fiber. With an oily, waxy base, it is somewhat wiry but blooms into a smooth, fluffy, breathable yarn that is great for knitting into lightweight cardigans and tops to wear in warm weather.

- Hemp

The hemp plant is especially versatile, and one of its few common applications is the use of its fibers for knitting yarn. The earthy roughness of hemp will mellow with time and use. The sturdy fiber is suitable for knitting openwork shopping bags and household items like tablecloths and coasters and is typically created in an environmentally responsible manner.

- Ramie

The fiber called ramie yields a plant from the nettle family. The plant's inner bark is transformed into fibers that have a luster but are a little brittle, so before being spun into yarn, they are usually mixed with other fibers. Ramie does not insulate well, as with other vegetable fibers, but it does create a breathable, sturdy fabric.

Scissors

Always have a pair of high-quality scissors available for clipping yarn ends and cutting off yarn. The best scissors are sharp, short-bladed ones because they allow you to cut precisely where you need to and cleanly complete a seam by trimming darned-in ends.

Knitting Needle Gauge

There are no size labels on certain knitting needles, such as double-pointed, circular, interchangeable, and antique needles. It is important to know what size a needle is, so poke it through the holes in the gauge to find out. Also included in several is a ruler you may use to measure gauge swatches.

Pins

On certain pins, the wide head stops them from being stuck in a piece of work. Use them when finishing work to pin bits of knitting together and when blocking to pin work out to the right measurements.

Stitch Holders

They are used to carry stitches too, which you will return later. A piece of lightweight cotton yarn, a safety pin, or a paperclip might make your stitch holder.

Stitch Markers

When working in a circle, use these to indicate the start and finish of the stitch panel and the completion of each row. Shift it from the left-hand to the right-hand needle when you arrive at a marker; continue working the row as usual.

Needle Organizer

Use this to keep your knitting needles sorted and safe from harm. In various types and sizes, needle rolls and bags are available. Thick needles (like a long pencil case) are ideally fit for a needle bag; double-pointed needles may be placed in a small needle roll.

Knitting Bag

Bags for knitters also have several compartments, ideal for storing your current project's tools and supplies. Keep a cedar cube inside to protect the knitting from dampness and moths.

Row Counter

Accessible as a tube at the end of a knitting needle: when you complete a row, change the counter; also, as a clicker that you "click" every time you finish a row.

Crochet Hook

Various materials, such as metal, bamboo, and wood, are available. A crochet hook makes it much simpler to pick up previously lost stitches. The slippery surface of the metal version theoretically makes this the most user-friendly type. You may use a crochet hook for attaching tassels as well.

Styles of Knitting

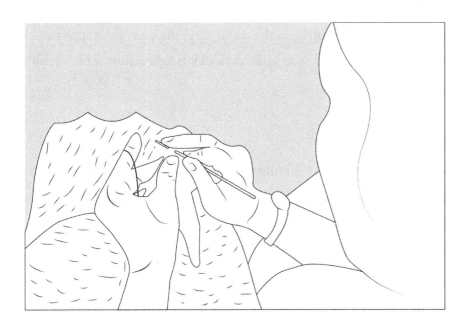

Continental Knitting

Continental knitting, originally common in Germany, is more efficient than English. It requires less movement than English knitting. Continental knitters hold both the yarn and needle in the left hand; thus, Continental knitting is often favored by left-handed knitters. In Continental knitting, the yarn is wrapped around the pinky, over the ring and middle fingers, and around the index finger of the left hand. The index finger is used to move and position the working yarn. The cast-on stitches are held in the left hand, and the right hand is the working needle.

Take the tip of the right-hand needle up and through the front loop of the first stitch on the left-hand needle. Bend your left index finger slightly to lower the working yarn and catch a loop of the yarn with the tip of the right-hand needle. Pull the loop and allow the stitch to slide off the left-hand needle. Move your index finger to adjust the tension on the yarn in your left hand and continue working to the end of the row.

If you are working flat or back and forth, you will need to turn the work to work the wrong-side row. The speed of Continental knitting is particularly helpful when working long areas of stockinette in the round. The minimal movement enables you to move quickly and easily through long stitching areas.

Eastern Knitting

Western-style knitting methods produce relatively flat knitting. In South America, Asia, the Middle East, and some parts of Eastern Europe, Eastern knitting often twists the stitches. The Eastern stitch sits on the needle differently because of how the yarn is wrapped, placing the left-hand leg of the knit stitch in front of the right.

While the needle is inserted into the stitch to form a knit stitch, in the same way, the yarn is wrapped over and forward, rather than backward, or in a clockwise rather than counterclockwise direction. This motion changes the orientation of the stitch on the needle.

Combined or Combination Knitting

Combined knitting relies upon a mixture of Eastern and Western knitting techniques. Some knitters find that a Combination style is faster, while others get a more even tension between knitting and purl rows when they choose Combination knitting over traditional Western knitting. In combination knitting, the purl stitches are worked Eastern style. This results in a twisted stitch; however, the knitter untwists each stitch during the following knit row.

Left-Handed Knitting

Both right and left-handed knitters can learn and master all knitting methods. Knitting is a two-handed skill, and approximately 50% of left-handed knitters knit, just like right-handed knitters. The remainder of left-handed knitters knits left-handed, reversing the instructions and using the left needle as the working needle and the right needle as the non-working one.

While this is effective, it can cause pattern reading challenges. Essentially, the left-handed knitter is knitting backward and will need to adjust patterns accordingly to correct the shaping, increases, and decreases. While this likely will not matter much for scarves and hats, it will make a big difference with sweaters and other garments that need to match on the left and right. If you are left-handed, you may want to experiment with left- and right-handed knitting. Some left-handed knitters opt to knit left-handed only when convenient or helpful, for example, to avoid turning their work.

Cable Knitting

Cable knitting involves crossing stitches over one another. Cables can be worked on stockinette, ribbing, or other simple stitch patterns. A cable can involve as few as two or as many as six to 12 stitches. Typically, cable knitting requires a cable needle. The cable needle is short, with a hump in the center or a curve at one end. A set number of stitches are moved from the left-hand needle to the cable needle and held to the front or back of the work, as directed by the pattern. The remainder of the stitches in the cable are knitted or purled, and then the stitches held on the cable needle are worked.

Cable knitting is typically charted with cables occurring at regular intervals. Carefully count or track your rows to make sure you place cables where needed. You will find cables in various patterns, like socks, hats, pillows, and heavy sweaters.

A simple cable occasionally twists to the left or right, forming a rope-like shape. Cables can open and close, moving around and across your knitting. More complex patterns may create florals, hearts, or Celtic-style knots.

Cable knitting can produce a relatively light or very dense fabric, but this knitting technique preserves the elasticity of the fabric. Cable knitting produces beautiful socks, sweaters, hats, and more.

Stockinette Knitting

It has been shown that knitting in stockinette stitch is among the best knitting patterns for beginners. This is a fundamental stitch to learn. Don't worry about getting a narrow gauge knit or a broad gauge knit. The finished knitting piece will be beautiful. You can use stockinette stitch for garments, which will still be beautiful. You can use it for a garment that is not even-textured, like a sweater.

In stockinette stitch, you always knit one row, then purl the next row. You knit most of each row on both sides. This pattern helps create ridges and valleys in the knitting. A 'ridge' will be when you do a stitch or a different pattern on one side of the knitting. A valley is when making a stitch pattern or different pattern on the other side of the knitting. A stockinette stitch has knit ridges and purl valleys on both sides.

Another important thing to know about the stockinette stitch is that brackets are at the beginning and end of each row. The brackets are blocky. These do not appear well on a stitch read from right to left. When it comes to a written pattern, the stitch read from the right side will be the purl ridges; the stitch read from left to right will be the knit ridges.

The single easiest place to find a knitting pattern like this is probably on a scarf pattern. For example, a scarf pattern may ask you to use 5mm knitting needles and stockinette stitches. If this pattern is on the first page of the pattern, there will be a few more steps. Some patterns like that have very complicated designs. If it is the last page of the pattern, it is at the end of the pattern. Look closely at the pattern you will be given, or go with the pattern that you are given. The instructions may tell you that you will be doing a stockinette stitch in rows and another kind of stitch in the other rows.

The stockinette stitch is a great stockinette knitting stitch. It is a stitch that can be worked by anyone and that anyone can use. It's the first of many stockinette stitches, the most common kind.

Lace Knitting

In simplest terms, lace produces knitting with an openwork pattern of increases and decreases. At its simplest, lace can be made with a yarn over, knit two-together pattern, creating a soft and open eyelet fabric. Lace knitting can produce flowing and interlacing floral and botanical patterns in their most complex forms. Lace, like other forms of relatively complex knitting, is usually charted. Simpler lace patterns are worked on right side rows and more complex ones on both right and wrong side rows. Lace patterns typically repeat across the width of your knitting.

You may find it helpful to use stitch markers or small rings to separate each chart, repeat, and track your work. Consider using a yarn needle to pass a contrasting heavy thread through your stitches every five to ten rows. This thread can enable you to save your work in the event of an error. Lace is typically not forgiving of mistakes and can be nearly impossible to rip out.

While many knitters think about fine, light pieces when looking at lace, lace can be worked in fine, laceweight yarns and sturdy, bulky yarns. The same pattern will produce a very different fabric worked in different yarns. A lace shawl worked in a heavy worsted yarn will be both lovely and cozy, while a laceweight shawlette will add a pretty accent to any outfit.

English Style

Knitting in English is achieved by keeping the yarn in your right hand. The patterns are formed on the piece's exterior (public-facing) face. Knitting English style (also known as 'throwing') is characterized by holding the yarn in your right hand and wrapping it around the needle. The movement can be subtle or deliberate, and there are countless variations of how your right-hand holds the yarn. English knitting is a style that includes keeping the thread, alongside the working needle, in the dominant hand. While it is popular in the British Isles and North America, knitting in English is done worldwide by knitters and is perhaps the most common. More than 60% said they knit English style in a survey of under 300 all Free Knitting writers.

Norwegian Knitting

The Norwegian knitting style is distinct due to how purl stitches are handled. This particular hold places the working yarn on the non-dominant side, making it a continental variant; the knit stitches are worked much like the standard continental type.

Russian Knitting

Russian knitting is very similar to standard continental knitting, and the knit and purl stitches worked similarly. The only difference with Russian knitting is that the working yarn is wrapped around the non-dominant hand's pointer finger, very similar to where it originates as the leading leg of the cloth. It makes a very close grip on the Russian style that helps you to flip the yarn over the tip of the needle instead of taking it with the needle itself. This technique is similar to kneading the lever with the yarn in the non-dominant hand.

Portuguese/ Incan/ Turkish Style

This method is done by holding the yarn around the neck or from a hook in the necklace type, enabling the knitter to knit on the opposite. Usually, patterns are produced by stranding the yarn outside the piece.

This knitting style is a real attention-getter— you tie the yarn to tension around your arm and flip the working yarn to create stitches with your thumb. Purl stitches are usually quicker with this style, so it's perfect on the wrong side to work stockinette in the round. Portuguese knitting is excellent since the yarn tension is not carried in the hands. Instead, Portuguese knitters tie the yarn around their necks—the rationale why numerous knitters like this style are because pace makes the fingers free up.

The tension is kept in the hands in every different knitting style; this provides two things for the hands to do simultaneously— keep the yarn and work the stitches with the needles. There's one less thing you must think about when making the stitches when the stress is kept around the arm. This technique is also perfect for helping with knitting discomfort since the yarn retains so much of the tension in the hands.

If you're not out of the way to knit with the yarn around your arm, you can also purchase a Portuguese pin that is added to your shirt and keeps the tightness there.

Stitches

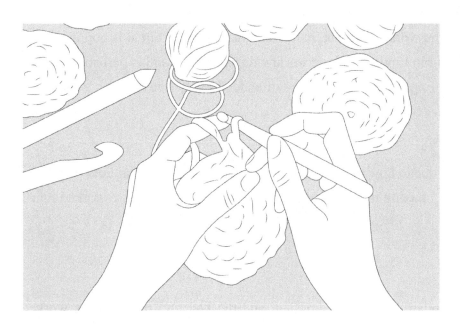

Knit Stitch

The rest is easy to follow if you have a clear concept of the knit cast-on. It's a very common and easy method for knitting and is always appreciated by new knitters for a smooth beginning. Most novices confuse themselves after creating the first row (though it's not the first row) with the cast-on method and remain clueless about the next step.

All you have to do is shift the stitched from the needle in the left hand to the empty needle in the right hand. Insert the right needle through the first stitch from the front to back and holding the working yarn (keep at the back) in the right hand, wrap it around the needle (counterclockwise), and pull it out from the stitch with a newly made loop. Repetition of the whole procedure will gradually move all the stitches from the left-hand needle to the right-hand one. While all the stitches will move, just flip your project and continue knitting.

Purl Stitch

You are no longer a novice. You have already begun knitting! Let's learn another way of stitching to make your work more interesting.

Like the knit stitch, the purl stitch is also one of the basic knitting stitches we can mention. The purl stitch looks like the opposite side of the knit stitch. If you continue with the purl stitch, you will get a bumpy texture on your project. For the purl stitch, keep the yarn at the front side of your work and insert the right needle through the first stitch of the left needle from right to left. The right needle must be wrapped around the yarn (counterclockwise). Create a new loop while pulling the needle out and slip one stitch from the left.

Slip Stitch Patterns

Before you are ready to tackle cables or lace, you can work with slip-stitch patterns. These offer a simple way to create highly textured and patterned knitting. Slip stitch patterns use two or more yarn colors; however, only one color is worked per row. The pattern is achieved by not working or slipping some stitches from the previous color as you work across the row. Simple slip stitches can create polka dots, checks, or a waffle knit pattern. Slip stitches create a rather bulky fabric, making them ideal for housewares like dishcloths and potholders.

Rib Stitch

Now you will learn a particular stitch that I believe you will use for the maximum time in your project. It is known as the rib stitch and is widely used in knitting sweaters, scarves and collars. This pattern needs extra care and concentration from the knitters, and you must also maintain the pattern. Usually, a 1*1 pattern is widely used, which means one knit stitch and one purl stitch. Keep the yarn back while doing the knit stitch and at the front while doing the purl. I will suggest keeping an even number of stitches for this pattern. If you have an odd number of stitches, you will know that you made a mistake somewhere along the way. Follow this pattern to get a beautiful texture: in the first row, one knit, one purl, and in the second row, one purl and one knit.

Though we have discussed a handful of stitching patterns for the beginner here, there are even more that we have not touched base on. These may not be perfect at this beginning stage, but you can practice them at the next level. You will find rib stitches, slip stitches, bobbles, eyelets, and many more to make your knitting experience thrilling and challenging. Now we will move to an entirely new segment of knitting.

Twisted Stitch

There are two types of twisted stitches: one you create purposely for design and one you have made by mistake. If you did this purposely, then it's very nice, but if not, then the trouble begins. In most cases, this is caused by stitches that slipped off the needle and were incorrectly placed back on the needle, resulting in twisted stitches. How will you know that? It's easy. They will never sit smoothly on the needle. One of the easiest ways of fixing them is to unravel them from the needle and put them back on, but you can fix them without removing them from the needle too. Just knit it from the back loop, and it will be untwisted.

Dropped Stitches

Dropped stitches are a common mistake made by every knitter, even experts, trying to concentrate on other things while knitting. Dropped stitches are a nightmare to those who have no idea how to fix them, but to those who do know how, the technique is as easy as any other. When you drop a stitch creates a long ladder of yarn on your knitted project, which can be scary for new knitters. I understand your feelings, but it is easy to fix with a crochet hook. First, identify the dropped stitch and place it on the crochet hook. At this point, you should remember that if you are dealing with a knit stitch, the ladder will remain behind the dropped stitch on the crochet hook and in front of the purl stitch. Insert the crochet hook through the dropped stitch, hook the yarn's last thread, and pull it out through the dropped stitch. Continue the process until you cover the entire missing rows, and finally, correctly place it on the working needle to avoid a twisted stitch.

Incomplete Stitches

An incomplete stitch occurs when the yarn is wrapped around the needle but not pulled through the stitch. For the knit stitch, insert the needle from back to front, pull the yarn through it, and place it on the left needle. For the purl stitch, just insert the needle into the stitch, and the rest is the same.

Back Stitch

This variation creates a twisted, ribbed effect and a beautiful texture. To begin:

1. Place the right needle into the back of the stitch on the needle in the left.

The following steps are the same as the basic knit:

1. Twist the yarn over the needle in your right hand.
2. A loop is created when you pull it through and slide the first stitch off the needle in your left hand.
3. Keep repeating Steps 2 and 3 until all the stitches have moved from the needle in your left hand to the needle in the right.

Seed Stitch

The seed stitch is often used in basic knitting, and it's just another type of stitch that you'll need to keep moving forward with your new hobby. It's essential to work each stitch opposite to the manner that it presents. For example, if the stitch was knitted in the previous row, you'll knit it. If it was purled, then you'll purl it.

- Step 1: Knit 1, and then Purl 1, and then repeat from to the very last stitch.
- Step 2: Continue to work each stitch oppositely that it presents; these rows will form your pattern.

Rib Stitch

This is also an incredibly easy stitch to make, and you'll be working the stitch in the manner it presents. For example, if the stitch was knitted in the first row, it'll present like a purl stitch in the next row. If the stitch were a purl stitch in the first row, it'd look like a knit stitch in the second. This means you'll be knitting the stitch if the previous row was purled and purling the stitch if the previous row was knit.

- Step 1: Knit 1 Stitch, and then Purl 1 Stitch. Repeat your pattern and go to the last stitch in the row.
- Step 2: You'll work each stitch in the manner it presents, as stated above.

Stockinette Stitch

This is a stitch pattern made of purl and knit stitches, and each row will alternate between the two. For example, one row will be purl, and the next will be knit, or vice versa. It's a trendy stitch pattern, and a gauge is usually measured based on a stockinette stitch pattern. It's as easy as follows.

- Step 1: Knit all of your stitches in this row.
- Step 2: Purl all of your stitches in the next row
- Step 3: Repeat for the desired length.

Garter Stitch

This is a pattern where you only use knit stitches or purl stitches. You will not be switching between the two. You'll knit or purl all the stitches in that row, and once you get to the end, you'll switch the needles around. This means that your working needles will become your holding needle and vice versa. It's that simple, and it's your most basic stitch pattern.

Eyelet Stitches

Eyelet stitches are a simple technique that produces beautiful results. It is effectively a small hole in the fabric, either purely for decoration or threading something through – like ribbon.

Here is an excellent guide for creating a basic eyelet stitch pattern:

- Knit one row at the length you desire.
- Purl the next row.
- Moving onto the third row, knit two stitches.
- Then yarn over, knit two stitches together, and knit one stitch.
- Repeat the steps in the point above until the end of the row.
- Purl the next row.
- Repeat all of these steps until the eyelet stitch is complete.

Tips and Tricks

Stick with Inexpensive Yarn

Though it sounds like a no-brainer, it's something that you should try out. You may get overwhelmed by all the choices when you pick up supplies. Some are definitely bound to be more expensive than others, and some are even harder to work with. Remember that inexpensive yarn, especially manmade yarn, is considered easy to work with, so it should be picked up first.

Knit with Others

Knitting with a friend is a great bonding activity, and it allows you something to do when you run out of inspiration or want a nice day or night with someone you care about. You can even exchange thoughts with one another and help when the other person is having trouble, making mistakes less likely to happen in the first place.

Organize Your Supplies

You may not be the most well-organized person in the world, but there should be some organization to your supplies if you want to knit without any added frustration. Constantly looking for something will frustrate you, and it may cause you to give up on a project entirely. You'll want everything where it's easily found and accessible. Having a knitting bag or basket beside you when you start is always a good recommendation, and having an organized one will be even better.

Get Curious About New Ideas

The beauty of knitting today is that there are many techniques and options for you to experiment with. As you are learning, now is a great time to try out some fun ideas. Give it a shot when you are following a pattern, and it throws a challenge at you. Directions for cables and yarns may scare you at first, but when you get into them, you will find they are not that bad. Plus, did you start knitting for just simple scarves? Probably not! So, this is the time to conquer your fear of a decrease and knit those beautiful hats!

Search for Inspiration and Enjoy Creativity

Scour Pinterest, stalk knitting blogs, and browse images of knitted projects to become inspired by what you will knit one day. Think about expanding your repertoire of knitting projects to include headbands, gloves, and other fun "newbie" projects. Many sites will allow you to search their pattern database by skill level to find projects you can complete at this stage and droll over projects you want to challenge yourself with as you keep practicing. This helps you find new projects, but when frustration and boredom kick in, you can scroll through your favorite places to reignite your dream of becoming a glorious knitter.

Just Keep Learning

Take the time to celebrate your accomplishment of reaching this coveted intermediate status, but do not let yourself stay here forever. You have worked so hard to learn the skills necessary to get here. Keep challenging yourself on new projects. Consider projects with more pieces or steps made of all challenging stitches or materials that are not generally associated with knitting (think plastic or beads). What can it hurt to give it a go?

Keep Your Stuff Where It Belongs

If you do not have a place for all your knitting supplies, now is the time to find a storage solution. Keep your yarn neat and tidy. Make sure your needles stay paired together. Do not lose all your stitch markers or yarn needles at the bottom of a bag or drawer. By this point, you know what your favorite needles and supplies are.

Find a Community

Coming into a group with only one skill level may seem like a good support group, but it will be hard to grow without the opportunity to learn and teach. Try to find a community that provides both for you. Plus, you will have some good laughs along the way at all the silly mess-ups made in all projects.

Try to Read Your Stitches

As you keep practicing and repeating projects, you will become more and more familiar with the look of the stitch variations. It may seem impossible to identify this initially, but you should be getting good at it by now. As you move through this intermediate stage, you will get even better. Before you know it, you might be reading your knitting to your kids as a bedtime story.

PART 1

KNITTING COLORFUL SOCKS

CHAPTER 1:
GAUGE AND TECHNIQUES

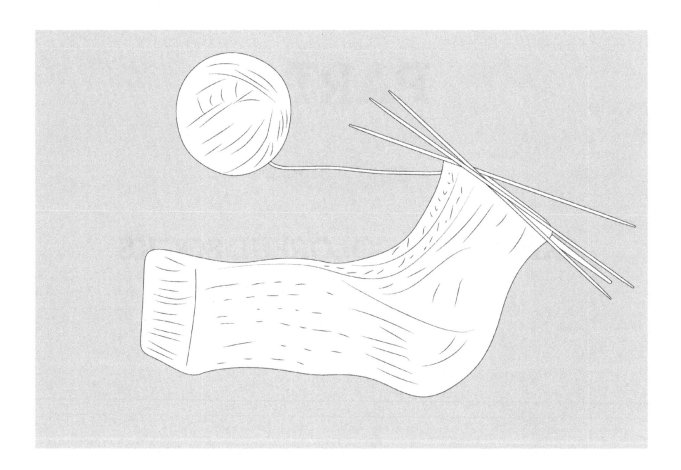

Gauge

Knitting Socks gauge swatch is so important as it helps you determine if the equipment you're using to knit with will create an end project the size you desire. Missing out on this step can result in the whole project coming out entirely of the wrong size. To complete the gauge, follow these steps:

- Stitches: Cast on the stitches required. It usually is 4 inches, plus six more stitches. So, for example. Suppose the gauge is given 18 stitches and 22 rows over 4 inches, cast on 24 stitches.

- Rows: Work in the stitch pattern specified for the number of rows required to make 4 inches plus six. Using the gauge specifications from the example above (18 stitches and 22 rows over 4 inches), you work in the given pattern of 28 rows.

- Bind Off: Finish the project and bind off loosely. Cut the yarn leaving an 8-inch tail.

- Measure: You'll then want to measure the swatch to check if the right number of stitches created the right size swatch. If not, you will need to change the needle size or yarn, or the result will be wrong. If you need more stitches per inch, you need smaller needles or thinner yarn, and if you need fewer stitches per inch, you'll want to change to bigger needles or thicker yarn.

Techniques

Increasing the Stitch

At any part of your knitting, you may need to increase the number of stitches to give your desired product a different shape. Several options are available to do so, and they are equally easy to handle. The first option is M1, generally used in the middle of a row to give an invisible increase. The second is an eyelet increase, equally popular among knitters, with the only drawback of leaving a hole behind. A moss increase is the third option. With this method, the newly made knit stitch remains on the left needle instead of being on the right needle. The list does not end here. We have ample options for completing the task, but they are not for beginners.

Tinking

If you have made any mistake in your working row or the row you have just finished, you can fix it by tinking. Tinking refers to undoing the stitches and returning to the wrong stitch to fix them. This technique is mainly used if the mistake is not too far back in work, as it is time-consuming and tiring to unravel and re-do a lot of work.

Decreasing the Stitch

Unlike increasing, sometimes we need to decrease the number of stitches to attain our desired shape. Different methods are used here also. As we have many different options, first decide which one to pick, and then execute your plan gradually. One option can be to knit two together, which means you merge two stitches and knit, considering two stitches as one. Another option is to purl two together, where the procedure is the same as before. Only use the purl stitch instead of the knit. Complicated methods such as knit return pass return, slip, slip, knit; slip, slip, purl, etc., are also available. With mastery of the skill, you can pick any one of these options to obtain your desired result.

Colorwork

Several types of colorwork exist, including intarsia, fair isle, and duplicate stitch. Intarsia and fair isle are knit, while the duplicate stitch is embroidered on the finished knitting project. Fair isle knitting is stranded colorwork, with multiple strands of yarn used across the row. Fair isle sweaters are a classic example. They have horizontal bands of patterned knitting. Intarsia knitting also uses multiple yarn colors, but they are worked in blocks to produce a design rather than across each row or round.

Depending on your chosen designs and patterns, colorwork can be fresh, modern, or traditional. It does have several drawbacks, particularly in terms of garment design. Fair isle knitting is relatively stiff, without a great deal of drape. The stranded knitting produces a very warm garment but is also quite dense. Intarsia knitting maintains its drape but must be worked with care to avoid potential gaping between the colors in work. Duplicate stitch has little bearing on the drape or weight of the knitting besides causing slight bulk.

Stripe Knitting

When it comes to knitting stripes or using two or more colors or types of yarn in a project, you must change colors or types at the end of every row. This is for you to ensure that your stripes are even and crisp.

Before you change yarn, make sure that you first get to cut the yarn with the original color and leave a few inches of tail. You will be able to use this for your later work.

Leave a few inches of the tail before adding the new color, and hold it tight. You can then begin knitting.

If you feel more comfortable with this technique, you may also try holding the original yarn's tail alongside the new yarn's tail.

The tricky part is that you will now be left with a couple of yarn tails because of all the times you have broken the yarn. You will have to weave this before you say your project is finished. Weave the ends into the same colors so your work looks organized.

Sizing

For store-bought socks, you have to choose the size that is the closest match to your foot. But when you are knitting socks, you can do a custom fit. Here are the measurements you need before you get started:

- Leg Length: The back of the leg, from where the top of the sock should be to the bottom of the heel.
- Cuff Circumference: Around the part of the leg where the cuff will be.
- Heel to Toe: The bottom of the foot, from the back of the heel to the end of the big toe.
- Toe Length: Just the toes.
- Foot Circumference: The part of the foot that is generally the widest, at the base of the toes.

CHAPTER 2:
PATTERNS AND PROJECTS

1. Adult Sock Pattern

Materials:

- US Size 1 needles (4 to 5 pairs of double-pointed needles)
- Yarn Needle or Crochet hook
- Stitch holder
- 1 skein (for women's sizes) or 2 skeins (for men's sizes) of yarn/465 yards.

Gauge:

- 32 sts, 48 r

Size:

- Adult

Instructions:

1. To make the leg, use the US 1 needles to cast on 68 using the long tail method. Arrange the stitches as evenly as you can on three double-pointed needles. Place the stitch holder and join. Do not twist the stitches.

- Knit 2, purl 2, ribbing until your piece measures 3 inches (7.5 cm). Keep working using a stocking stitch until your piece measures 8 inches (20.5 cm) or your desired length.

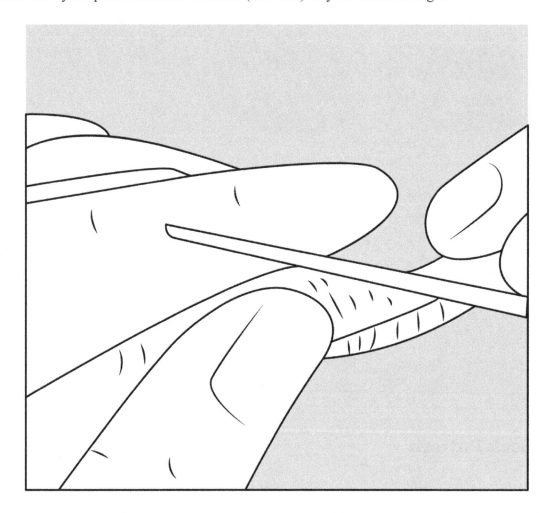

- To make the heel, knit across 17 stitches. Turn your work and purl across 34 stitches.
- Place 34 instep stitches on a spare needle or stitch holder and work them later.

2. Using the eye or partridge stitch pattern, begin the heel flap. Work back and forth on the heel stitches like this:

- Row one: Slip one purlwise with yarn in the back. Knit one and continue to end.
- Row two: Slip one purlwise with the yarn on the front. Purl to end.

3. Repeat rows 1 and 2 until you have 34 rows. You should have 17 chain selvage stitches on both edges of the project.

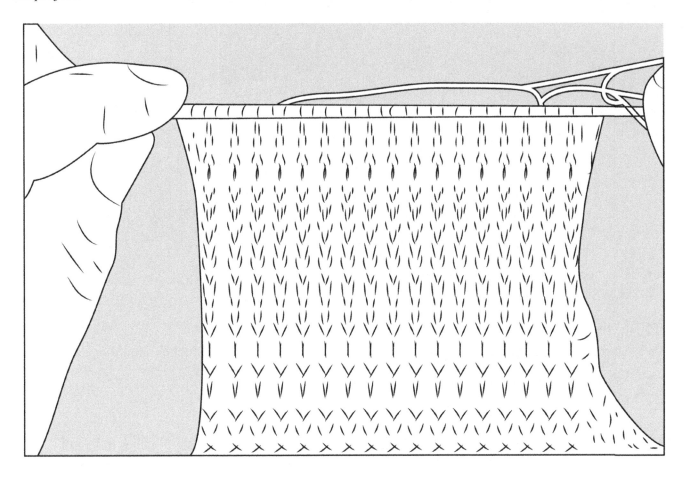

4. For the turn, heal, do the following:

- Row 1: Knit across 19 stitches, slip-slip-knit, knot 1. Turn the project over.
- Row 2: Slip one purlwise, purl 5, purl two together, purl 1, and turn.
- Row 3: Slip one purlwise, knit one stitch before the gap, slip-slip-knit with a stitch on each side of the gap, knit 1, and turn.
- Row 4: Slip one purlwise, purl to 1 stitch before the gap, purl two together (with one stitch from each side of the gap), purl 1, and turn.
- Repeat rows 3 and 4 until all the heel stitches are worked. End in row 4.

5. For the Heel gusset, knit across all heel stitches, and with double-pointed needles (needle 1), knit 17 stitches along the selvage edge of the heel flap.

- With double-pointed needles (needle 2), work them across the instep stitches from earlier.
- With more double-pointed needles (needle 3), knit 17 stitches along the other side of the heel and knit across half of your heel stitches. You should have a total of 88 stitches.

5. For the center back heel, round 1 will be:

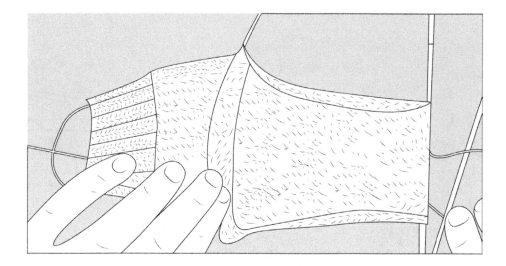

- Use needle 1 to knit to the last three stitches on needle 1.
- Knit 2 together, knit 1.
- Knit across all the instep stitches on needle 2.
- Starting at needle 3, knit 1, slip knit, and knit to the end. Two gusset stitches should be decreased.
- For round 2, knit.
- Repeat rounds 1 and 2 until you have 68 stitches.

7. For the foot, work using a stocking stitch pattern until your project measures 6.5 inches in length.

8. For the toe, do the following for round 1:

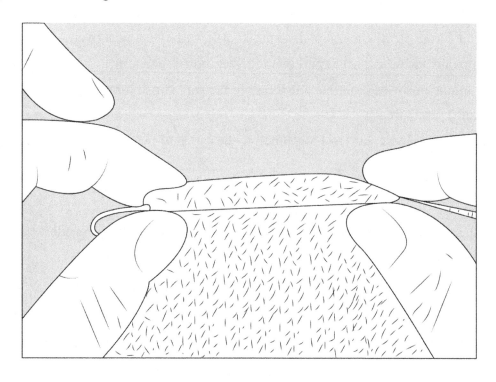

- Needle 1 knit to the last three stitches, knit two together, knit 1.
- For needle 2, knit 1, slip knit, knit to the last three stitches, and then knit two together.
- For needle 3, knit 1, slip-slip-knit, and knit to the end. For round 2, knit.
- Repeat rounds 1 and 2 until you have 32 stitches. From there, only repeat round 1 until only 12 stitches remain.

9. Knit the stitches from needle one onto needle 2. You should have six stitches on both needles.

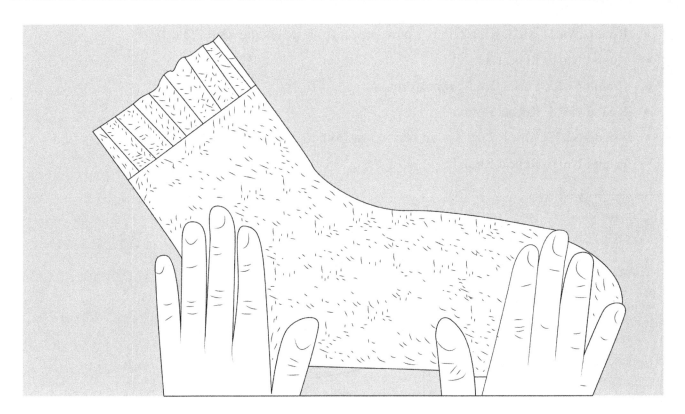

- Cut your yarn, leaving an 18-inch tail. Knit the two sides of the toe together and sew the loose ends. You are done!

2. Tube Socks

Materials:

- Yarn: 2 skeins of Fingerling weight yarn
- Needles: Size No. 1 U.S. (2 ¼ mm) needles (double pointed)/set of four
- Size No. 3 U.S. (3. ¼ mm) needles (double pointed)/set of four

Gauge:

- 7 stitches = 1 inch in stockinette stitch

Instructions:

- Use smaller needles, Cast on 36 stitches.
- Divide these stitches over three needles, then join.
- Knit 2, purl two, and rib stitch for 2 inches.
- Now, change to large needles and start the spiral pattern.

For the Spiral Pattern:

- Round No. 1: Purl1, Knit 2, Purl 2 now, repeat from to, ending Knit 2, Purl1
- Round No. 2: Repeat Round 1
- Round No. 3: Purl 2, Knit 2 repeat from to
- Round No. 4: Repeat Round 3
- Round No. 5: Knit 1, Purl 2, Knit two repeat from to, ending Purl 2, Knit 1
- Round No. 6: Repeat Round 5

- Round No. 7: Knit 2, Purl 2 repeat from to
- Round No. 8: Rep Round 7
- Repeat these eight rounds for 6½" (or desired length).

Shape Toe:

- Round No. 1: At the beginning of each needle, Knit 1, Slip 1, Knit 1, pass slipped stitch over, knit to last three sets of Knit 2 together, Knit 1

- Round No. 2: Knit across.

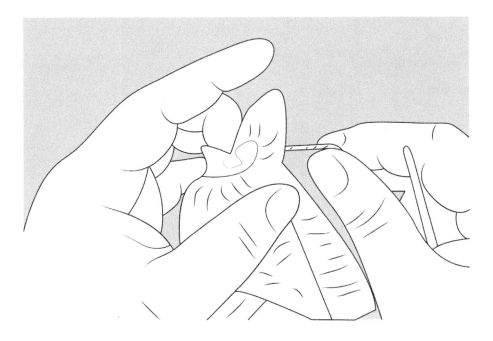

- Repeat these two rounds until 12 stitches remain. Knit 2 together around.

- Cut yarn and thread through the remaining sets. Pull to close and weave in the end on the Wrong Side.

3. Blasted Toe Socks

Materials:

- Yarn: 100 yards of worsted-weight yarn.
- Needles: Size No. 3 double-pointed needles.
- Stitching marker
- Safety pins or stitch holder
- Tapestry Needle

Gauge:

- 20 stitches = 4 inches in Stockinette stitch

Instructions:

- Cast on 34 stitches.
- Divide these stitches among the four double-pointed needles, then join.
- Now place the marker and mark the start of round

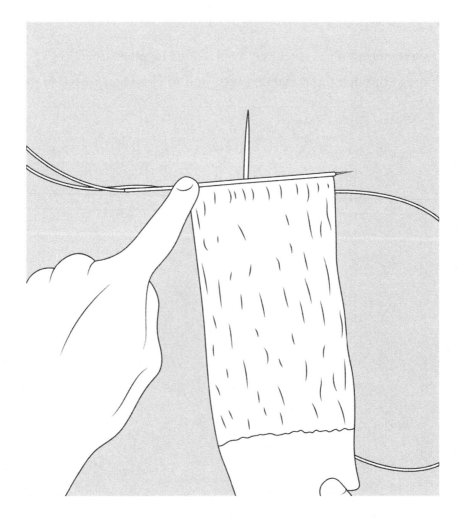

- Rounds 1 – 10: Knit through back loops. Purl 1 repeat this to stitch marker.
- Rounds 11 – 40: Knit across.
- Round 41A: Shape the toes. Knit 11 sets, cast on three more stitches, place the next 12 stitches on the holder (for this, use safety pins), and then knit the remaining 11 stitches back to the start of the round.
- Now you should have around 25 stitches divided on the double-pointed needles.
- Rounds 42A – 45A: Knit around 25 stitches evenly.

- Rounds 46A – 50A: Now Purl 1, Knit through back loops, Purl 1 repeat to marker.
- Now bind off those sets loosely.
- Round 41B: Shape the big toe by knitting across those 12 stitches on the holders and on three more stitches, which you cast on following the three sets of 41. Now place the marker.
- Rounds 42B –45B: Knit 15 stitches evenly.

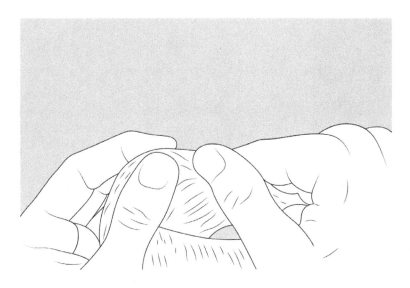

- Round 46B: Now knit two together, purl 1, Knit through back loops, purl one, repeat from to stitch marker.

- Rounds 47B – 50B: Now Knit through back loops, purl one repeat to marker.

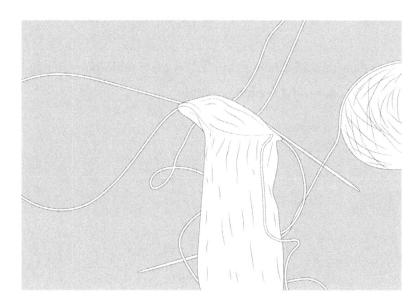

- Bind off these 14 stitches loosely.

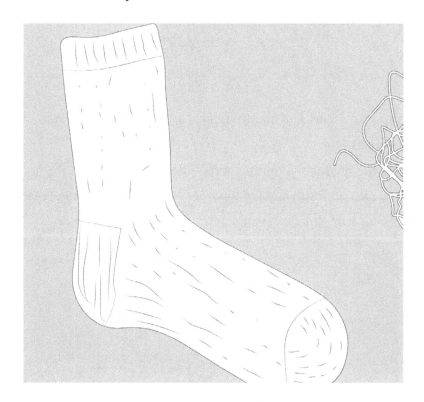

- Now repeat all this for the second sock.

Finishing:

- Weave in the ends using the tapestry needle.

4. Air Raid Socks Pattern

Materials:

- Yarn: 100 grams of variegated worsted-weight yarn.
- Needles: Size No. 1 double-pointed needles.
- Tapestry needle.

Gauge:

- 9 stitches = 1 inch in stockinette stitch.

Instructions:

- Cast on 60.
- Knit 1 through back loops, 1purl 1 around. Continue (raised ribbing) for 1/2 inch.
- Rows 1 – 2: Knit 4, purl 2. Repeat across.

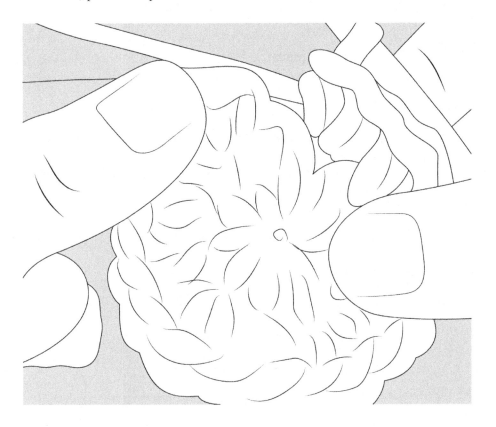

- Rows 3 – 4: Knit 3, purl 3. Repeat across.
- Rows 5 – 6: Knit 2, purl 4. Repeat across.
- Rows7– 8: Knit 1, purl 4, knit two repeats from to, ending with knit 1.
- Rows 9 – 10: Knit 1, purl 3, knit 3, repeat from to, ending with knit 2.
- Rows 11 – 12: Knit 1, purl 2, knit four repeats from to, ending with knit 3.

- Repeat until you get to the point where the sock leg reaches 7 or 8 inches in length (or as desired.)

Work the Heel:

- Heel Row 1: Knit 30. Now turn work.
- Heel Row 2: Slip 1, Purl 1, and then repeat.
- Repeat these rows 15 times (or desired length).
- Turn the Heel
- Row No. 1: Slip 1, purl 17, purl two together, purl 1. Then turn work.
- Row No. 2: Slip 1, knit 6, slip knit, knit 1. Then turn work.
- Continue until every heel stitch is complete.

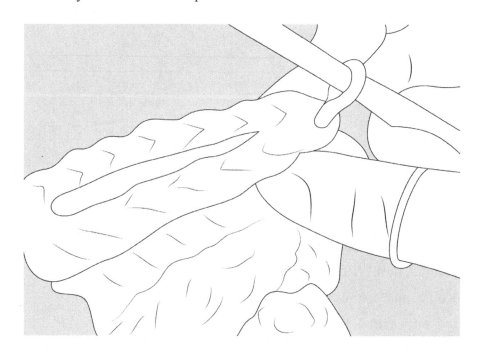

For the Gusset:

- Pick and knit around 15 stitches alongside the heel flap.
- Now knit across in the pattern as set.
- Then pick and knit 15 stitches again.
- Now knit one more row around. (Upon the instep stitches, continue the pattern)
- Now knit one slip knit, then knit to the remaining three stitches before instep, knit two together, and knit 1.
- Continue rows No. 1 and 2. Now decrease every other row and work pattern on the instep until you reach around 30 stitches at the foot. This way, continue in the pattern till the foot is about two inches below the desired length.

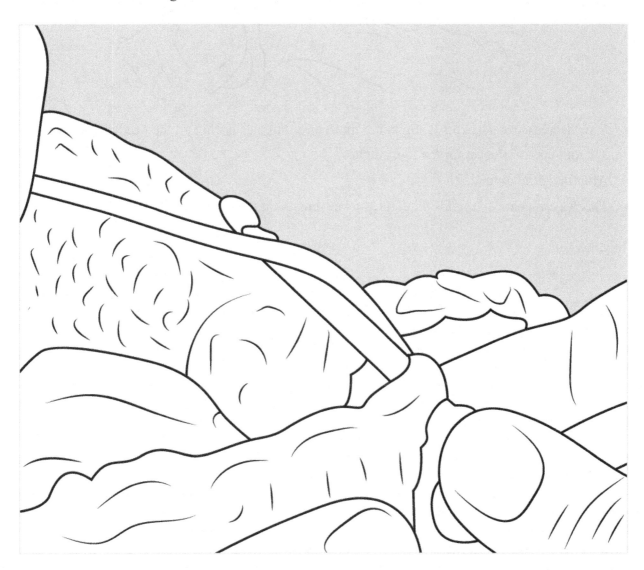

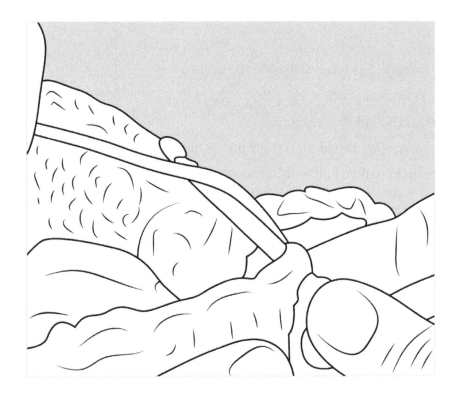

- Now decrease rounds: knit 1, slip knit, knit to three stitches lasting on the needle, knit two together, and knit across. Repeat for the foot stitches.
- After that, knit around.
- This way, repeat two rounds till eight stitches remain on the instep needle, now 16 stitches together.

Grafting the Toe:

- Weave it in all the ends. Repeat for the second sock.

5. Simple Sock Pattern

Materials:

- Needles: US 1 or 2.5 mm, double pointed to circular are recommended
- Yarn: Lightweight, fingerling weight, about 420 yards or about three balls
- Extra: Stitch markers, a gusset for heel shaping

Gauge:

- Gauge: 32 S for 4 inches using stocking stitch

Instructions:

- Create the cuff:

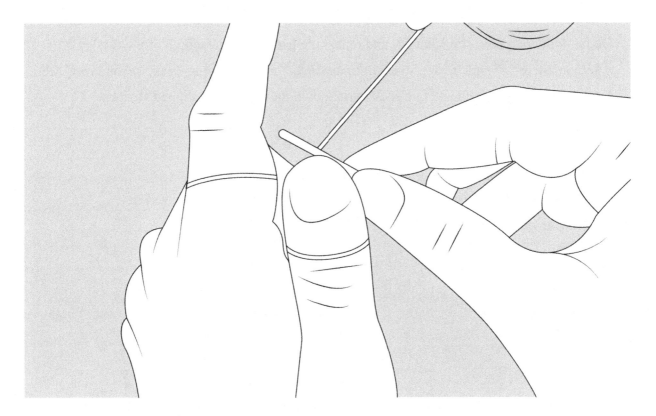

- Cast on 64 stitches, join working in the round, and mark with a stitch holder to mark the start of the row.
- Knit 1, purl 2, and knit 2. Repeat the 2-x-2 rib pattern (purl two and knit 2) until the last 3
- stitches. Purl 2 and knit 1.
- Repeat Step "b" until the work is 1.5 inches.
- To ensure it is even on the second sock, write down the number of rounds the ribbing was worked.
- On the next row, knit 1, purl 3, and repeat the pattern for the length of the row.

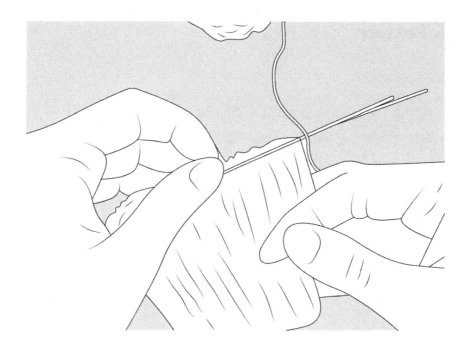

- On the following row, slip 1, knit 3, and repeat the pattern for the length of the row.
- Alternate Steps "e" and "f" until the work measures 7 inches, ending on the second row, Step "f."
- To ensure it is even on the second sock, write down the number of slipped stitches.

2. Create the heel flap:

- Row 1: Knit 16, turn the work over, slip 1, and purl 31.
- Make sure all your stitches are on one needle before beginning the next series.
- Row 2: Slip one and knit 1, repeating the pattern across the row.
- Row 3: Slip one and purl

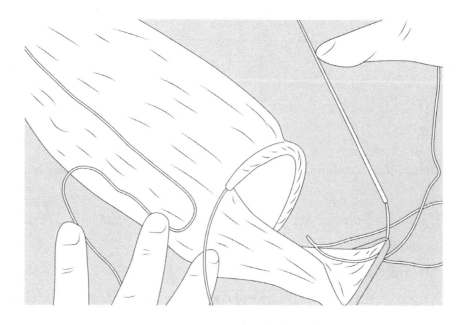

- Alternate Steps "c" and "d" for 16 times.

3. Turn the heel:

- Row 1: Slip 1, knit 18, slip, slip, knit, knit 1, and turn the work over.
- Row 2: Slip 1, purl 7, purl two together, purl 1, and turn the work over.
- Row 3: Slip 1, knit 8, slip, slip, knit, knit 1, and turn the work over.

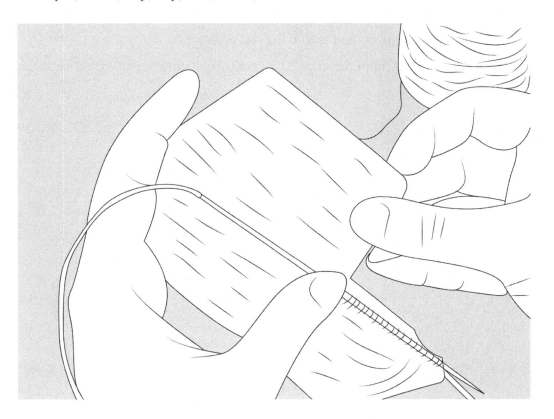

- Repeat Steps "a" through "c," adding one more stitch before every decrease until each stitch has been worked. This is about 20 stitches on the needle.

4. Create the sock:

- Knit 20 stitches, pick up and knit 17 stitches. Place a stitching marker.
- Knit 1, purl 3, and repeat for 32 stitches.
- Pick up and knit 1.

Place a stitching marker.

- Pick up and knit 17 stitches to the gusset area.
- Knit 10 stitches to the heel's center.

5. Create the gusset:

- Row 1: Knit 3 stitches with the stitching marker, then knit two together, knit 1, and slip the marker. Begin repeating knit one and purl 3 for the next 33 stitches. Slip the marker and knit 1, slip, slip, knit, and then knit the rest of the row.
- Row 2: Knit to the first stitching marker and slip the marker. Begin repeating knit 1, purl 3 for the next 31 stitches, slip the marker, and knit to the end of the row.
- Alternate Steps "a" and "b" until there are 32 stitches for the insole. This is 63 stitches
- altogether.

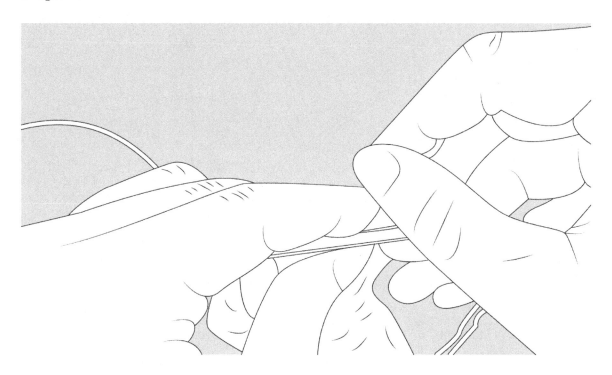

- Continue working, shaping down until about 2.5 inches longer than your desired length.

6. Create the toe:

- Begin by knitting to the first marker and slip the marker. Repeat knit 1, purl 3 for 31 stitches, then knit two together, slip the marker, and knit to the end of the row.
- On the next row, knit one across the row.

7. Create the toe shape:

- Row 1: Knit across until three stitches remain before the first marker. Knit two together and knit 1. When you slip the marker, knit 1, slip, slip, knit, and knit to within three stitches of the second marker.
- Knit 2 together, knit 1, slip the marker, knit 1, slip, knit, and finish the row.
- Row 2: Knit across the whole row.

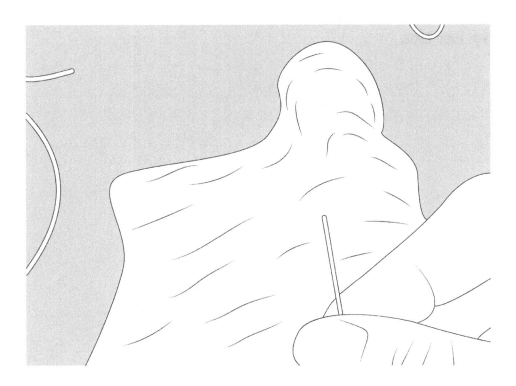

- Repeat Step "a" 4 additional times, decreasing until 16 stitches remain.
- Knot across the first marker, changing the stitches on your needle so that the stitches for the instep are on one needle and the insole is on your other needle.
- Trim the yarn, leaving a 16-inch tail.

8. Create/finish the sock:

- Using the yarn needle, sew the two sides together using a whipstitch.
- Trim the ends and intertwine them into the project.
- Repeat for the second sock.

6. Easy Baby Booties

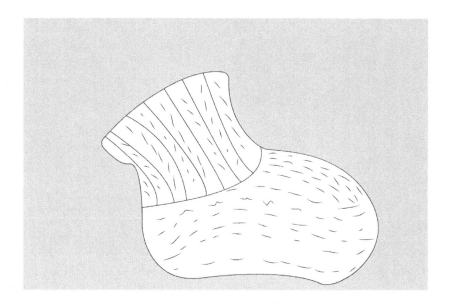

Materials:

- Medium-weight yarn (80 yds)
- Size 8 straight needles

Gauge:

- 26 S x 32 R

Size:

- 4 inches

Instructions:

- Create 26 stitches. Then, work in 10 rows of garter stitches.

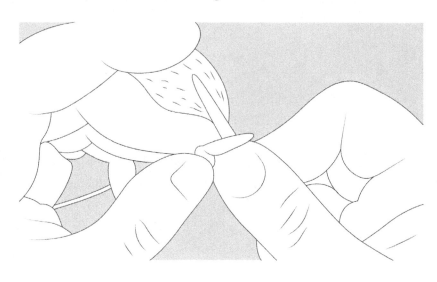

- Bind the ten stitches at the beginning of that next row, then finish it.
- Bind off ten stitches at the beginning of your new row. You should have six stitches in the middle. Use the garter stitch for an additional 20 rows instead of the six stitches in the middle. Then, bind off.

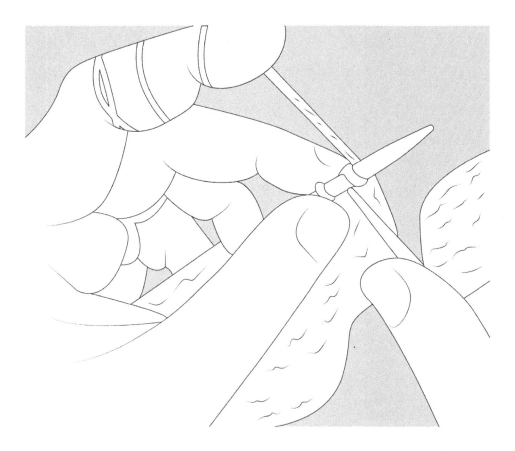

- You now have a T shape that you will use to wrap into the booties. The top part of the T shape is the back and side of your bootie, while the long, narrow part is the footbed.

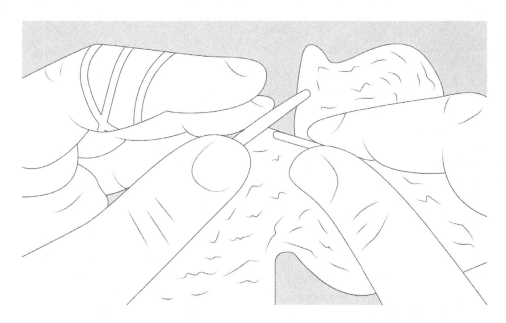

- Take one side of your back and place it on the footbed. Then, take the other side of the back and pull it over the other way. They are now crossing over each other into a cute bootie shape.

- Then, sew the bootie with a yarn needle, following the toes and sides. When done, turn the booties inside out to finish.

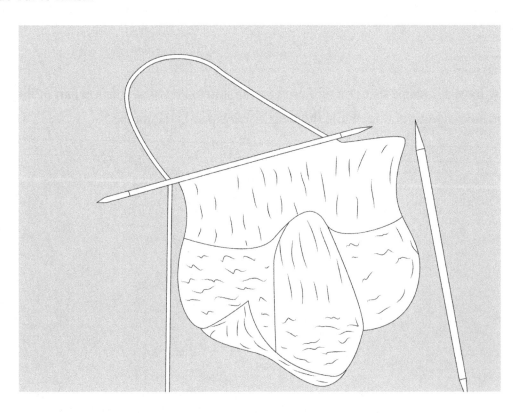

- Repeat the process a second time to create two booties.

7. Long Socks

Materials:

- 3 (3, 4, 4) skeins of Posy, including 75% super clean merino, 15% cashmere, and 10% nylons, each skein is around 318 yards/100 grams; roughly 630-645 (880-900, 1015-1045, 1175-1185) overall lawns required. We used Teal Twilight.
- A collection of people 0 dual sharp needles
- A stitch marker

Keep in mind, if making the Junior size for a Woman's United States 5-foot or smaller size, you will need two skeins of Posy.

Gauge:

- Fifty stitches and 48 rows = 4 inches in 2 × 2 Rib, unstretched.
- 28 stitches = 4 inches in 2 × 2 Rib, lengthened.
- 34 stitches and 50 rows = 4 inches in stockinette stitch

Dimensions:

- Junior (Adult Small, Adult Medium, Adult Large)
  - Cuff Circumference: 6 3/4(8, 8 3/4, 9 1/4) inches unstretched, quickly extending to 12(14 1/2, 15 1/2, 16 1/2) inches.
  - Foot Circumference: 5 1/4(6 3/4, 7 1/2, 8 1/2) inches unstretched, conveniently extending to 6 3/4(8 3/4, 9 3/4, 10 3/4) inches.
  - Foot Length: Adjustable.
  - Lower leg Length from top involving Heel to the top implying Cuff (unfolded): 18 (21, 21 3/4, 23 1/4)inches

Note: Slide all slipped stitches purlwise unless the pattern suggests otherwise.

Final Foot Length:

Younger Sizes:

- United States dimension 1Y (European 32) = 7 3/4 inches.
- US size 2Y (33) = 8 inches.
- United States size 3Y (34) = 8 1/2 inches.
- US size 4Y (36) = 8 3/4 inches.
- United States size 5Y (37) = 9 inches.
- United States size 6Y (38) = 9 3/8 inches.
- US dimension 7Y (39) = 9 5/8 inches.

Ladies Sizes:

- The United States' dimension of designing footwear, likewise, Europeans is (European 35) = eight 3/8 inches.
- US size 5 shoe (36) = 8 5/8 inches.
- United States dimension 6 footwear (37) = 9 inches.
- US dimension 7 footwear (38) = 9 1/4 inches.
- United States dimension eight shoes (39) = 9 5/8 inches.
- US dimension 9 footwear (40) = 10 inches.
- United States dimension 10 footwear (41) = 10 3/8 inches.

Men's Sizes:

- United States dimension seven shoes (European 39) = 9 5/8 inches.
- United States dimension 8 footwear (40) = 10 inches.
- US dimension 9 shoe (42) = 10 1/2 inches.
- United States size 10 shoe (43) = 10 3/4 inches.
- United States dimension 11 footwear (44) = 11 inches.
- US size 12 shoe (45) = 11 1/2 inches.
- US dimension 13 shoe (46) = 11 3/4 inches.

Instructions:

For the Cuff:

- Cast 84 (100, 108, 116) stitches onto three dual sharp needles. [Needles An and also C: 28 (34, 36, 38) stitches; Needle B: 28 (32, 36, 40) stitches]

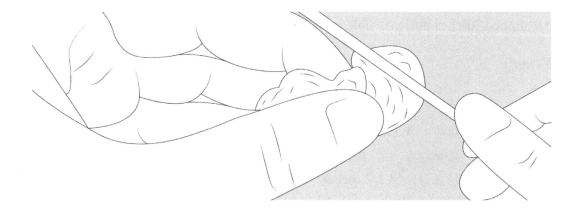

- Position the pen and join for working in the round, being careful not to turn the stitches.
- Round 1: K1, p2, k2, repeat from to last three stitches, p2, k1.
- Repeat Round 1 till piece procedures 9 (10, 10, 11) inches from the cast-on edge

For the Leg:

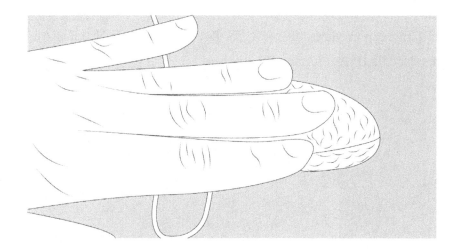

- Round 1: K1, p2, k2, repeat from to last three stitches, purl two with each other (p2tog), k1. [1 stitch lowered] Round 2: K1, p2, k2, repeat from to last two stitches, knit 2 with each other (k2tog). [1 stitch reduced] Round 3: K1, p2, k2, repeat from to last five stitches, p2, k1, k2tog. [1 stitch minimized] Round 4: K1, p2, k2, repeat from to last four stitches, p2, k2tog. [1 stitch cut] Round 5: K1, p2, k2, repeat from to last three stitches, p2, k1.

- Repeat Round 5 8 (11, 12, 13) a great deal, even more times.

- Round 6: K1, p2tog with the back loophole (TBL), k2, p2 repeat from to the last stitch, k1. [1 stitch lowered] Round 7: Slip slip knit (SSK), k2, p2, repeat from last stitch, k1. [1 stitch decreased] Round 8: Ssk, k1, p2, k2, repeat from to last three stitches, p2, k1. [1 stitch lowered]

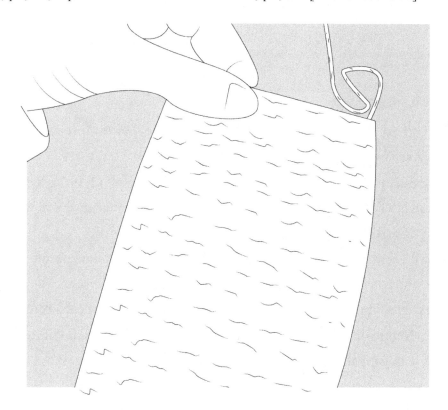

- Series 9: Ssk, p2, k2, repeat from to last three stitches, p2, k1. [1 stitch cut]
- Repeat Round 5 9 (12, 13, 14) many more times
- Repeat Round 1 three more times. [52 (68, 76, 84) stitches total; Needles An as well as C: 12 (18, 20, 22) stitches; Needle B: 28 (32, 36, 40) stitches]

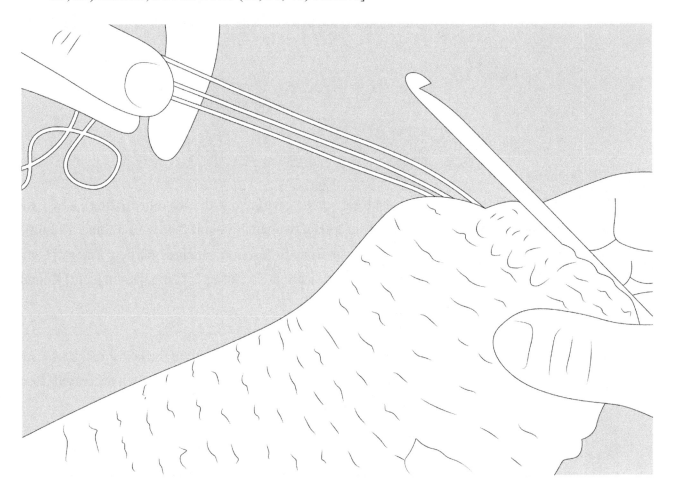

For the Heel Flap:

- Set-Up Row 1 (best side): K1, [p2, k2] 3 (4, 4, 5) times, p0 (0, 2, 0), turn job so wrong side is encountering you.
- Set-Up Row 2 (side): K0 (0, 2, 0), [p2, k2] 6 (8, 9, 10) times, p2 (2, 0, 2). Keep In Mind: These 26 (34, 38, 42) stitches are the start of the Heel Flap, and also, for this area, you will function to and fro on these 26 (34, 38, 42) stitches.
- Organize stitches so that 26 (34, 38, 42) Heel Flap stitches get on one needle and continue to stitch to get a hold on various other two needles: 13 (17, 19, 21) stitches each.
- Work following rows to and fro, the transforming job in Intervals of each row.
- Row 1: Slip 1 (Note) with yarn in back (WYIB), k1, repeat from the end of row.
- Row 2: Slip 1 with yarn ahead (WYIF), purl to finish of row.
- Repeat Rows 1.

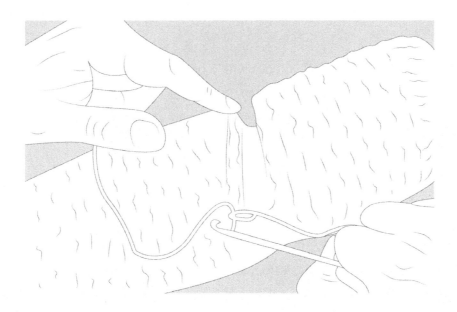

For the Heel:

- Row 1 (ideal side): K15 (19, 21, 23) SSK, k1, turn job so wrong side is encountering you, and also there are 17 (21, 23, 25) stitches on the left needle and even 8 (12, 14, 16) stitches on the suitable needle.

- Row 2 (wrong side): Slip 1, p5, p2tog, p1, turn work. [16 (20, 22, 24) stitches on the left needle as well as likewise 8 (12, 14, 16) stitches on the best needle] Row 3: Slip 1, knit to 1 stitch before space, SSK (with the suture before the void, also, to sew after the gap), k1, turn work.

- Row 4: Slip 1, purl to 1 stitch before a gap, p2tog, p1, turn work.

- Repeat Rows 3 and, likewise, four up until all Heel stitches have functioned. [16 (20, 22, 24) Heel stitches stay]

For the Gusset:

- Weave across 16 (20, 22, 24) Heel stitches with a brand-new needle (currently called Needle A).
- With Needle A, get and also knit 13 (18, 19, 20) stitches along Heel Flap. [29 (38, 41, 44) stitches on Needle A] With new needle (currently called Needle B), k0 (0, 2, 0), [p2, k2] 6 (8, 9, 10) times, p2 (2, 0, 2).
- With a new needle (now called Needle C), grab in addition to 13 (18, 19, 20) stitches along Heel Flap.
- With Needle G, knit 8 (10, 14, 12) stitches from As an example A. [68 (90, 98, 106) total stitches; Needles An and also C: 21 (28, 30, 32) stitches; Needle B: 26 (34, 38, 42) stitches] Round 1: For Needle A, knit to last three stitches, k2tog, k1; for new Needle B, k0 (0, 2, 0), [p2 - k2] 6 (8, 9, 10) times, p2 (2, 0, 2); for Needle C, k1, SSK, knit to complete of a needle. [2 stitches reduced] Round 2: For Needle A, knit to end of needle; for Needle B, k0 (0, 2, 0), [K2, p2] 6 (8, 9, 10) times, p2 (2, 0, 2); for Needle C, knit to finish of the needle.

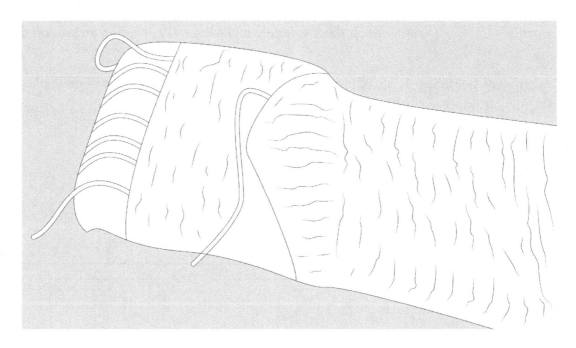

- Repeat Rounds 1 as well as two until 52 (68, 76, 84) stitches remain. [Needles An as well as C: 13 (17, 19, 21) stitches; Needle B: 26 (34, 38, 42) stitches]

For the Foot:

- Round 1: For Needle A, knit to finish of needle; for fine Needle -B, k0 (0, 2, 0), [p2, k2] 6 (8, 9, 10) times, p2 (2, 0, 2); for Needle C, knit to end of the needle.
- Repeat Round 1 till Foot procedures 1 1/4 (1 3/4, 2 1/4, 2 1/2) inches much less than the preferred final length, gauging from the back edge of the Heel. Below's how long you'll desire the last Foot length.

For the Toe:

- Set-Up Round: Knit to finish off the round.
- Round 1: For Needle A, knit to last three stitches, k2tog, k1; for Needle B, k1, SSK, knit to last three stitches, k2tog, k1; for Needle C, k1, SSK, knit to complete a needle. [4 stitches reduced]
- Rounds 2-- 4: Knit to end off the series.
- Repeat Rounds 1-- 4 one (2, 3, 3) many more times. [44 (56, 60, 68) stitches]
- Repeat Rounds 1 and 2 three (3, 3, 4) times. [32 (44, 48, 52) stitches]
- Repeat Round 1 2 (3, 4, 5) times. [24 (32, 32, 32) stitches] With Needle C, knit the 6 (8, 8, 8) stitches from Needle A, so there are 12 (16, 16, 16) stitches on each of the two needles.
- Use Kitchener Stitch to graft the Toe closed.

Finish:

- Weave in the long run, and then make another sock!

Block both socks by soaking them in hot-temperature water, squeezing the excess water, and laying them flat to dry. To clean socks, either equipment clean and cool and topple completely dry low or hand laundry with mild soap in a container or space temperature water.

8. Children's Socks

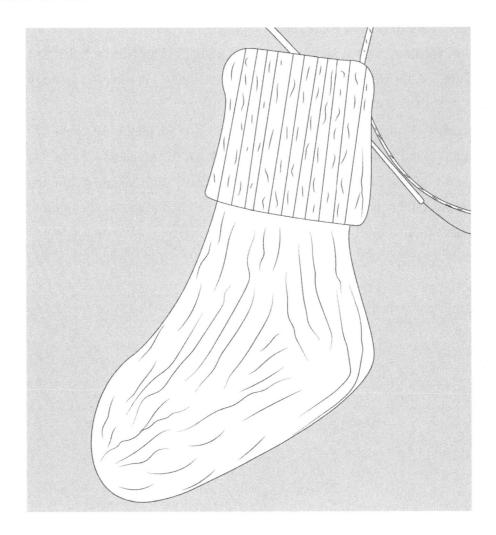

Materials:

- Size: Hell to toe is 6.5 inches.
- Yarn: 2 balls of size four yarn in 2 colors.
- Needles: Size 2 double-pointed needles.
- Tools Required: Yarn, needle.

Gauge:

- 32 stitches and 42 rows = 4 inches.

Instructions:

For the Cuff:

- Cast on 48 stitches
- Distribute these over the needles and join in the round

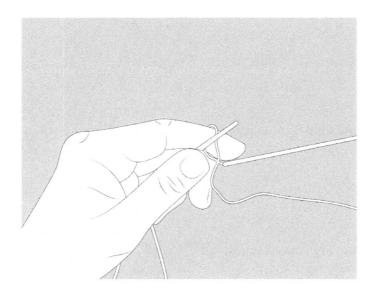

The leg of the sock is worked in the rib stitch – knit 1, purl 3. Use this for the following rounds:

- ten rounds in the main color
- six rounds in the 2nd (contrasting) color
- six rounds in the main color
- four rounds in the 2nd color
- six rounds in the main color
- two rounds in the 2nd color
- eight rounds in the main color

For the heel flap, purl one stitch onto the previous needle

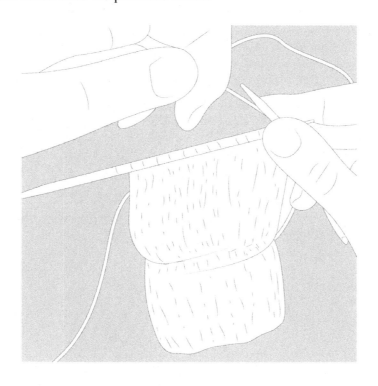

Then for the first row:

- Slip one stitch
- Knit 22 stitches

Turn your work (put the remaining 25 stitches onto spare two needles or a stitch holder)

For the second row:

- Slip one stitch
- Purl 22
- Repeat these two rows eight more times

For the Turn Heel:

Row 1:

- Slip one stitch
- Knit 14
- Slip slip knit
- Knit 1
- Turn the work

Row 2:

- Slip one stitch
- Purl 7
- Purl 2 together
- Purl 1
- Turn

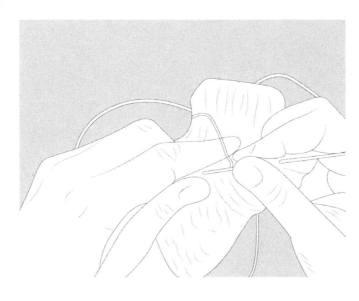

Row 3:

- Slip one stitch
- Knit 8
- Slip slip knit
- Knit 1
- Turn

Row 4:

- Slip one stitch
- Purl 9
- Purl 2 together
- Purl 1
- Turn

Row 5:

- Slip one stitch
- Knit 10
- Slip slip knit
- Knit 1
- Turn

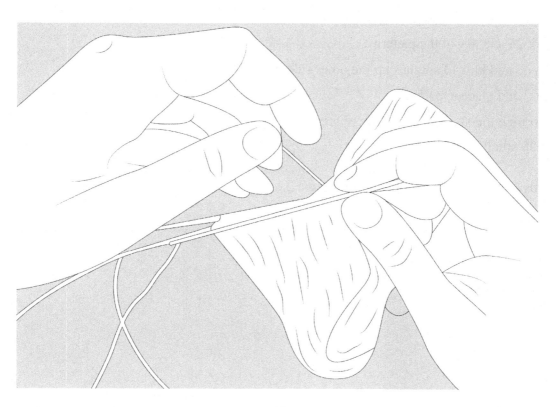

Row 6:

- Slip one stitch
- Purl 11
- Purl 2 together
- Purl 1
- Turn

Row 7:

- Slip one stitch
- Knit 12
- Slip slip knit
- Turn

Row 8:

- Purl 13 stitches
- Purl 2 together
- Purl 1

For the Instep:

- Knit 15 stitches of the heel
- Knit 13 stitches down the edge of the heel
- Work 25 stitches of the pattern
- Pick up and knit 13 stitches up the other side of the heel
- Knit 7 and place a marker
- Rearrange the stitches so that there are 21 on the 1st needle, 25 pattern stitches on the 2nd needle, and 20 stitches on the 3rd.

Knit 6 rounds, continuing the rib pattern on needle 2

Using needle 1:

- Knit to the last three stitches
- Knit 2 together
- Knit 1

Using needle 2, work the rib pattern

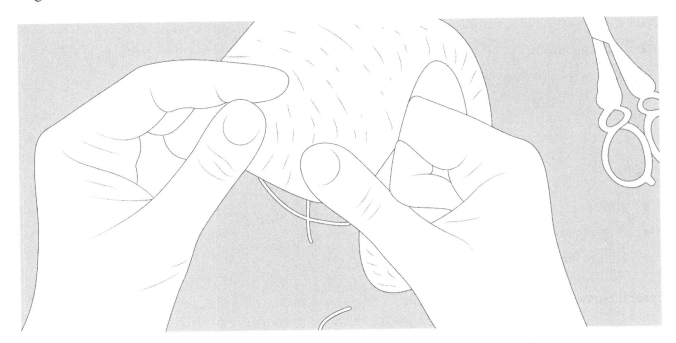

With needle 3:

- Knit 1
- Slip slip knit
- Knit to the end of the round

Knit with needles 1 and 3

Knit the rib pattern with needle 2

Repeat all of this five more times

Continue without decreasing until the foot measures approximately 1½ inches

For the toe, use the 2nd color

End off the rib pattern on needle 2

For the first round, knit on all needles

For the Second Round:

Using needle 1:

- Knit until the last three stitches
- Knit 2 together
- Knit

Using needle 2:

- Knit 1
- Slip slip knit
- Knit to the last three stitches
- Knit 2 together
- Knit 1

Using needle 3:

- Knit 1
- Slip slip knit
- Knit to the end

Repeat these two rounds five more times

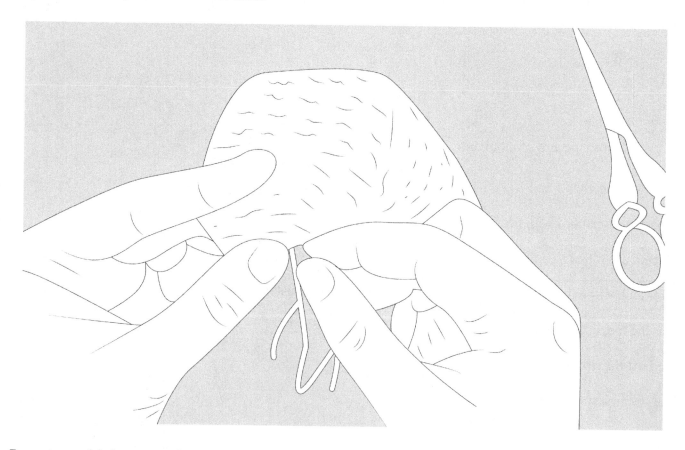

Repeat round 2 four more times

Bind off and sew in any ends

9. Beginner's Sock Knitting Pattern

Materials:

- 2 Skeins Knit Picks Swish DK Yarn (50 Grams, 112 Meters/123 Yards); Color 'Jade'
- 1 Set Size U.S. 3 (3.25 Mm) Double Pointed Needles
- 1 Stitch Marker
- Tape Measure
- Large-Eyed Yarn Needle
- Scissors

Gauge:

- 6 Stitches And 9 Rows Equal 1 Inch In Stockinette Stitch

Finished Measurements/Sizes:

- Small/Medium: Cuff Circumference, 7 Inches; Length, Variable; To Fit Women's U.S. 6 To 8 Shoe Sizes.
- Medium/Large: Cuff Circumference, 8 Inches; Length, Variable; To Fit Women's U.S. 9 To 11 Shoe Sizes.

Note: The finished fabric has a fairly high degree of stretch. The pattern first gives small/medium instructions, followed by medium/large in parentheses. Be sure to follow the numbers for your chosen size.

Instructions:

For the Cuff:

- CO 42 (48) stitches and join for working in the round, being careful not to twist.
- Round 1: k2, p1*, repeat from to * around.
- Round 2: k all stitches

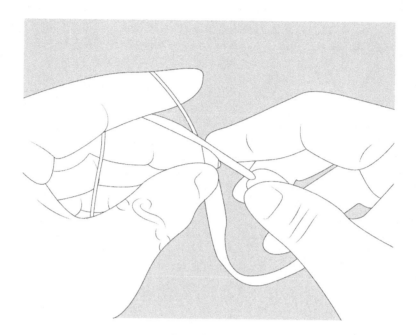

- Repeat these two rounds six times more than work round 1 again -- 15 rounds total. (Note: for a longer cuff, work more 2-round repeats, being sure to end after working a round 1.) Do not work the last stitch of the last round. Turn work. The heel is worked back and forth over the previous (20) 23 stitches. The remaining (22) 25 stitches are left unworked until gusset.

For the Heel Flap:

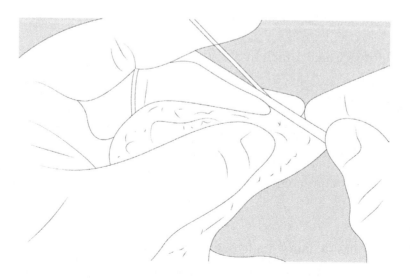

Note: Stitches are slipped purlwise with yarn held to the front of the work.

- Row 1 (WS): Slip 1, p to last stitch, k1tbl.
- Row 2 (RS): Slip 1, k1, p1, k2* to last three stitches, p1, k1, k1tbl.
- Repeat rows 1 and 2 (8) 9 more times, ending ready to work a wrong side row ([18] 20 rows worked in total).

For the Turn Heel:

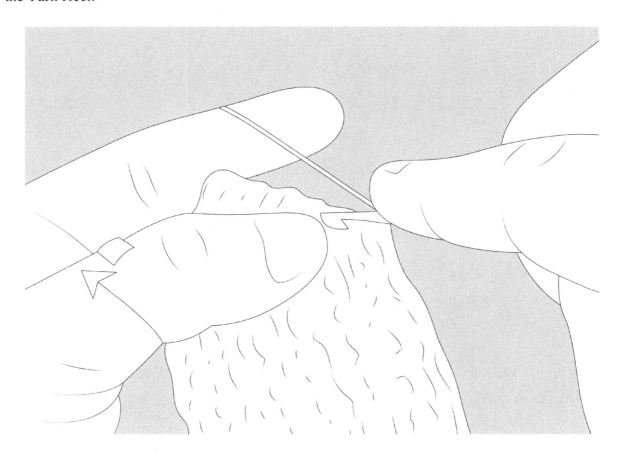

Small:

- Row 1: Sl 1, p11, p2tog, p1, turn
- Row 2: Sl 1, k5, ssk, k1, turn
- Row 1: Sl 1, p6, p2tog, p1, turn
- Row 2: Sl 1, k7, ssk, k1, turn
- Row 3: Sl 1, p8, p2tog, p1, turn
- Row 4: Sl 1, k9, ssk, k1, turn
- Row 5: Sl 1, p10, p2tog, turn
- Row 6: Sl 1, k10, ssk
- 12 stitches remain

Large:

- Row 1: Sl 1, p13, p2tog, p1, turn
- Row 2: Sl 1, k6, ssk, k1, turn
- Row 3: Sl 1, p7, p2tog, p1, turn
- Row 4: Sl 1, k8, ssk, k1, turn
- Row 5: Sl 1, p9, p2tog, p1, turn
- Row 6: Sl 1, k10, ssk, k1, turn
- Row 7: Sl 1, p11, p2tog, p1, turn

- Row 8: Sl 1, k12, ssk, k1
- 15 stitches remain

For the Gusset:

- Pick up and knit (9) 10, make one extra stitch in the corner – (10) 11 stitches picked up the total. This is now Needle 1.
- Knit across (22) 25 stitches on the instep needle. This is now Needle 2.
- Make one stitch in a corner, pick up and knit (9) 10, knit (6) 7 from Needle 1 onto this needle (Needle 3). Needle 1 has (16) 19 stitches; Needle 2, (22) 25; Needle 3, (16) 18.
- Round 1: Knit all stitches on Needle 1. Needle 2: p1, k2*, repeat from to * to last stitch, p1. Knit all stitches on Needle 3.
- Round 2: Needle 1 -- knit to last three stitches, k2tog, k1; Needle 2 -- knit all stitches; Needle 3 -- k1, ssk, knit to end of the needle.
- Repeat rounds 1 and 2 until (42) 48 stitches remain.
- Work until the foot measures 1.5 inches less than the desired length.

For the Toe:

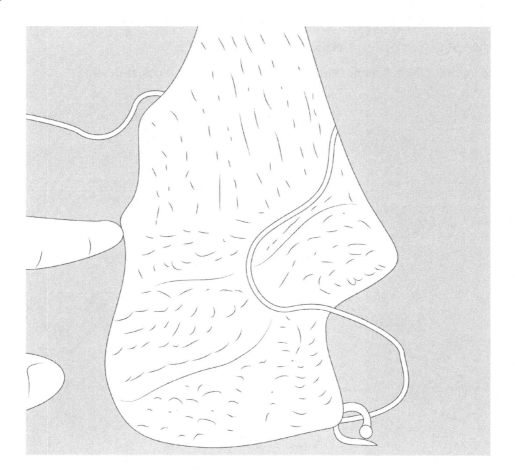

Note – before beginning the toe, shift one stitch from Needle 2 to Needle 1 and one from Needle 2 to Needle 3 (size small) or shift one stitch from Needle 2 to Needle 3 (size large).

- Round 1: Needle 1 -- knit to last three stitches, k2tog, k1; Needle 2 -- k1, ssk, knit to last three stitches, k2tog, k1; Needle 3 -- k1, ssk, knit to end of a needle.

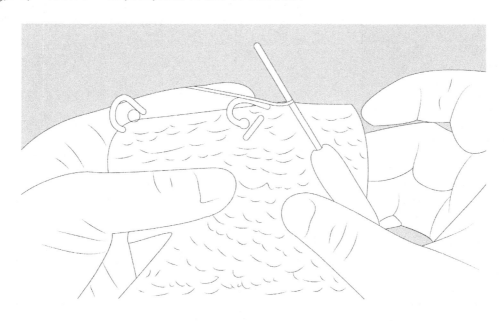

- Round 2: Knit all stitches.

- Repeat rounds 1 and 2 until (20) 24 stitches remain. Work only round 1 until (10) 12 stitches remain. Knit stitches from Needle 1 to Needle 3.

- Finish the toe with the Kitchener stitch. Weave in ends and block if desired.

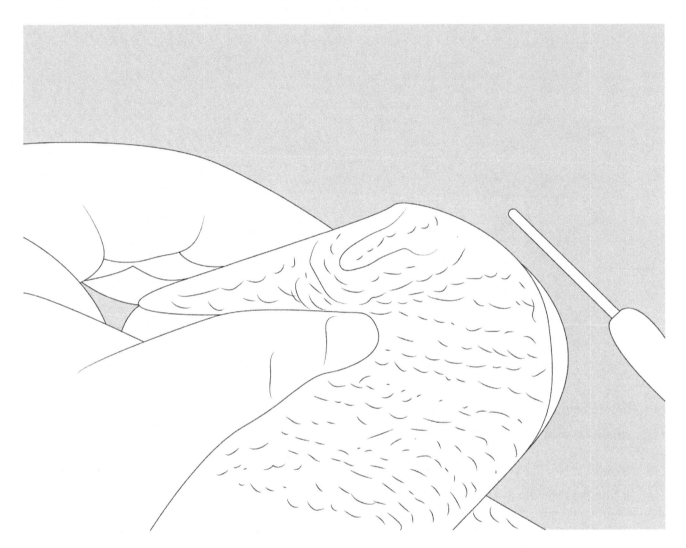

PART 2

KNITTING COLORFUL HATS

CHAPTER 1:
GAUGE AND TECHNIQUES

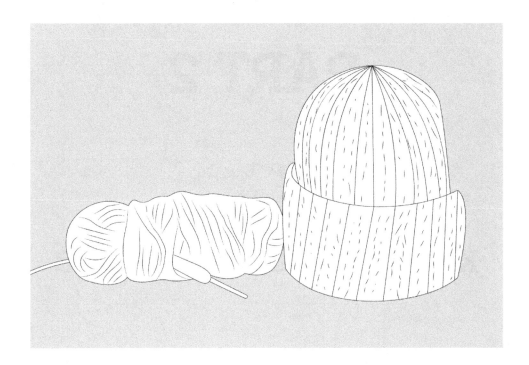

Gauge

Understanding gauge is critical to your hat knitting success. Gauge is the number of stitches and rows per inch in your knitting, typically measured over four inches of knitting. If your gauge is off, your garment will be too small or too large, causing frustration. If the gauge is too loose, it can also result in significantly more yarn usage, even when the fit is not an issue. Fitting a garment, from a sweater to a hat, requires matching the number of stitches suggested per inch in the pattern.

Knitting patterns include the gauge, which is written as two numbers. For example, if the gauge is listed as 20 stitches and 24 rows over four inches, a 4-inch by 4-inch swatch will have 20 stitches in each row and 24 rows total, or five stitches and six rows per inch. If you are knitting too tightly and getting 24 stitches per 4-inches, the garment will be much smaller than the designer intended, while if you are getting 17 stitches per inch, it will be too large.

Before you start a project, you should knit a gauge swatch. The gauge swatch is a 4-inch to 6-inch square, worked in the same pattern as the final knitting project. If your pattern calls for you to knit a flat stockinette, you should knit one row and purl one row throughout your gauge swatch. Ribbing, lace, and cable knitting should also be worked in a pattern. You may wish to knit every row for four rows at the top and bottom of a stockinette or pattern swatch to keep it flat and make it easier to measure.

To knit a gauge swatch, look at the suggested gauge and divide it by four. If the pattern requires 24 stitches over four inches, you will need six stitches per inch. Cast on enough stitches to produce a 6-inch square, in this case, 36. Knit a square, working in a garter, stockinette, or pattern as your knitting pattern requires. Bind off the stitches. Pin the square to a flat surface, like an ironing board, and measure with a hard ruler, marking 4 inches on the square with straight pins. Carefully count the stitches and rows.

If you have too many stitches, make another gauge swatch using a needle one or two sizes larger. Use a needle one to two sizes smaller if you have too few. With time and practice, you will recognize your knitting tendencies and develop some idea of your gauge. While gauge swatches remain important, you will likely have a better idea of whether you need to choose a different needle size.

Most gauge swatches can be pinned and measured as soon as knitted; however, a few yarns may require additional care. These yarns should be washed, blocked flat, and measured. In most cases, this sort of care is only required for sweaters or other very large projects. If careful measurements are essential, many patterns will note specific blocking instructions for the gauge swatch or that the gauge should be measured after blocking.

Depending upon the yarn, you may wish to unravel your gauge swatches, use them as pockets, craft them into other items, or save them for future reference. If you opt to save them, pin a note with the yarn and needle size to the swatch.

While gauge swatching is essential for wearables, it is less critical for other projects. Scarves, dishcloths, and pillows are typically usable whether they meet gauge or not. In the case of a dishcloth, the finished product is only slightly larger than a gauge swatch. Simply use your best judgment for these projects and choose a needle that produces an appealing fabric with your yarn.

You should get in the habit of swatching because as your skills grow, your gauge may change. Even if you have been a tight knitter, you may relax with practice, or a loose knitter may tighten up over time. Changing how you knit from continental to English may impact your gauge, as can injuries, fatigue, and the type of needles and yarn.

Techniques

In any knitting, size matters. It is critical in a hat. A little extra length in the sleeve or room around the stomach can be acceptable on a sweater. But when you guess wrong with the size of a hat, an inch makes a huge difference!

One of the advantages of knitting a hat is being able to size it exactly to the head that will be wearing it. Not everyone is a standard size, so paying attention to the measurements assures the perfect fit. If you have ever had to squeeze a hat over your head or, conversely, had it slip over your face, you know that "one size fits all" doesn't apply here.

There are two measurements you need when knitting a hat:

- Circumference: Measure where the hat will start on the head. This could be the forehead for something to be pulled down to just above the eyes or higher up on the hairline for a beret or slouch cap.
- Height: Measure from the bottom point where the hat will sit to the crown of the head.

Remember that these are the actual head measurements. When knitting, you will add to the height of the hat, depending on how much additional room you want there. For the circumference, you want the hat to sit comfortably, not stretched to the max to fit.

Choosing Your Materials

Knitting Needles

Hats are usually knitted in the round. That means there is no seam because you knit round and round in a circle, not back and forth, on a straight needle. You will be using a combination of circular needles and double-pointed needles.

Circular needles are two single-pointed needles that are connected by a cable. The cable length varies. The wider the piece you knit, the larger the cable you need. For hats, you will use a 16-inch circular needle to get started. Once you start decreasing the crown of the hat, the circumference of the hat will get smaller than 16 inches, so you will need to switch to double-pointed needles (sorry, they do not make itty-bitty cables for circular needles).

Double-pointed knitting needles are precisely that. They are pointed on both ends. This allows you to move end-to-end, from needle to needle. Yes, it seems odd at first, but invest in learning the technique because you will use it in many other projects that require knitting a piece with a small circumference, like socks, mittens, gloves, and the sleeves and necklines on sweaters.

In addition to the type of needle (circular and double-pointed), you need to choose the kind of material your needles are made from. Needles can be plastic, aluminum, nickel-plated, wood (walnut, rosewood, cherry, birch), and bamboo (it is a plant, not wood). Let me just say that no one should knit with plastic needles. Sure, they come in fun colors, but plastic needles bend, which also means they break. And who needs more plastic in their life?

Choosing the Correct Yarn

Once you have chosen your pattern, the next step is to decide on the yarn. To avoid re-calculating your stitches, you should note the weight category specified in the pattern (e.g., Worsted, Bulky). Another important consideration is the yarn's fiber. Wool is warm but can be itchy, depending on the type of wool. Shetland, for example, is rough, but merino is wonderfully soft and is often referred to as the cashmere of wools. Mohair is made from goat fibers, and while it looks fluffy, it can be quite itchy on the head.

Some softer natural animal fibers include alpaca, llama, cashmere, angora, and silk. You can also choose natural plant fibers, including bamboo, soy, linen, cotton, and hemp.

Animal fibers tend to hold their shape better than plant fibers. If you have ever had a cotton sweater pushed up the sleeves, you know it doesn't spring back to shape easily or ever. That's because, unlike plant fibers, animal fibers have microscopic hooks, like Velcro, that hold them together and provide more protection for the animal. You might hear yarn aficionados talk about "fiber memory". They refer to the ability to retain the shape. If you knit a hat from cotton or bamboo, it will likely stretch, so consider that when making your choice and deciding on the size.

You might also come across a label that says "Superwool" or "Washable Wool". This wool fiber has been treated to avoid the fiber's natural inclination to shrink when tossed in a washer or dryer. Washable wool is a great hat fiber choice for someone who would not want to bother with hand-washing or dry cleaning.

In addition to natural fibers, you will discover a wide range of manmade fibers, like acrylic, Tencel, nylon, and viscose. These fibers add bling to the yarn: the shiny, sparkly, fuzzy, stretchy, textured looks that can make hats colorful and fun.

Textured and multi-colored (variegated, self-patterning) yarns are great for dressing up a simple hat pattern like the Rolled Brim Hat featured later in this book. With this yarn, you just knit and let the yarn do the chic stuff.

If you are knitting a hat with a pattern stitch (like the Spiral Ribbed Hat featured later in this book), choose a non-textured yarn that will showcase your stitching.

Finally, ensure the yarn will provide the look you have wanted for a long time. Pay attention to the care instructions so you are not investing your knitting time into a hat that will need tender, loving care because it will either not be worn or rarely be cleaned, and trust me, a hat needs regular cleaning.

Weave in Ends

Weaving in ends is the first way that you can try to finish your project. The main goals are that you get to hide the ends of the yarns, prevent the yarns from unraveling, which would damage your finished product, and make the product look nice and good to see. Plus, if it is a piece of garment you are creating, then weaving in ends would make it more comfortable to wear.

Before you close the loops, make sure that you could leave around six inches of yarn first. Then, start with a new ball of yarn at the end of your product and avoid putting lots of thread in places where it's not supposed to be added.

You can also try holding both strands of yarn while still ensuring that you leave at least six inches of it behind and then knit the next stitch while holding the said strands of yarn together. This will result in one bulky stitch and one normal one but do not worry because this will not be noticeable if you have done it right.

Work on the stitches on the wrong side of the piece and use the purling method to do this. You can weave across or diagonally; whichever you are comfortable with is fine. You may also try duplicating stitches. Just follow through with what you have already started and then make the same stitches to cover up what is wrong and secure the sides of the project.

Blocking

Blocking makes your knitting take the shape you want it to. Blocking supplies can be as minimal as your ironing board, and some pins or can involve foam mats, wires, and more. Blocking is typically used for wool and plant fibers. Traditional methods cannot block acrylic yarns.

To block your knitting, gently soak it in lukewarm water. You can opt to wash it with a mild shampoo or a wool wash designed for hand knitting. Avoid using hot water or agitating your knitting, especially if you have worked in wool or another animal fiber.

Remove the knitting from the soaking water and blot excess water with a clean, light-colored towel. Be incredibly gentle if you are working with lace or very lightweight yarn. Sturdier projects can be rolled in a clean towel and pressed to remove moisture.

Place the damp knitting on a flat surface large enough to accommodate it. Hats and small scarves can be blocked on an ironing board, while large sweaters and shawls require the space of a bed or a significant area of the floor. Ideally, choose a warm spot away from pets and children with good ventilation.

Lay the item out flat, stretching it as needed. If the pattern has provided dimensions, match the garment's size to those dimensions at this time. Pin the item into place to hold it while it dries.

CHAPTER 2:
PATTERNS AND PROJECTS

1. Pompom Winter Hat

Materials:

- Simply Soft (170 g/6. oz;288 m/315 yds); Contrast A Neon Yellow (9773) - 1 ball
- Simply Soft Heathers (141 g/5. oz;228 m/250 yds); Main Color (MC) Charcoal Heather (9508) - 1 ball
- Sizes U.S. 7 (4.5 mm) and U.S. 8 (5 mm) circular knitting needles 16" [40 cm] long
- Set of four sizes U.S. 8 (5 mm) double-pointed knitting needles or size needed to obtain gauge
- Stitch marker

Gauge:

- 18 sts and 24 rows = 4" [10 cm] in stocking stitch with larger needles and one strand.

Instructions:

- With two strands of MC tog and a smaller circular needle cast on 88 sts. Join in the round, placing a marker on first st.

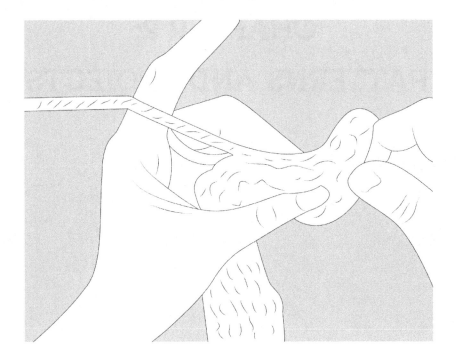

- 1st round: Knit.
- 2nd round: Purl.
- Repeat the last two rounds until the beginning measures 2½" [6 cm], ending on a knit round.

For the Latvian Braid:

- 1st round: With two strands of MC, K1. With 2 strands of A, K1. Repeat from around.
- 2nd round: With MC and A held in front of work, With MC, P1. With A, P1. When switching yarns, wrap yarn for the next st under yarn used for the previous st. Repeat around.

- 3rd round: With MC, P1. With A, P1. When switching yarns, wrap the yarn for the next st over the yarn used for the previous st. Repeat around.
- Break A and one strand of MC.
- With the remaining one strand of MC and a larger circular knitting needle, knit in rounds until work from the beginning measures 6" [15 cm].

Shape top, changing to set of 4 double pointed needles where appropriate:

- 1st round: K9. K2tog. Repeat around. 80 sts.
- 2nd and alternate rounds: Knit.

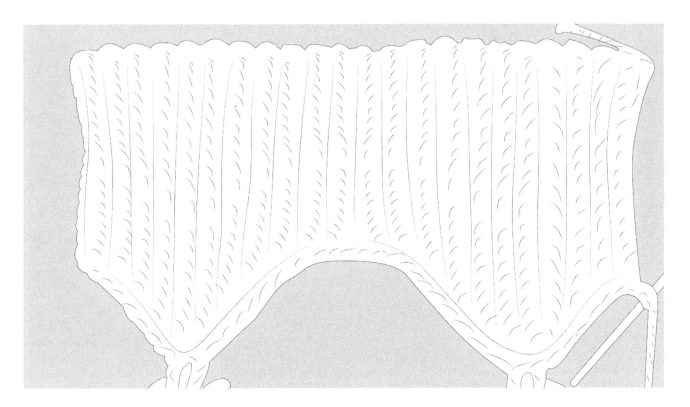

- 3rd round: K8. K2tog. Repeat around. 72 sts.
- 5th round: K7. K2tog. Repeat form around. 64 sts.
- 7th round: K6. K2tog. Repeat from around. 56 sts.
- 9th round: K5. K2tog. Repeat around. 48 sts.
- 11th round: K4. K2tog. Repeat around. 40 sts.
- 13th round: K3. K2tog. Repeat around. 32 sts.

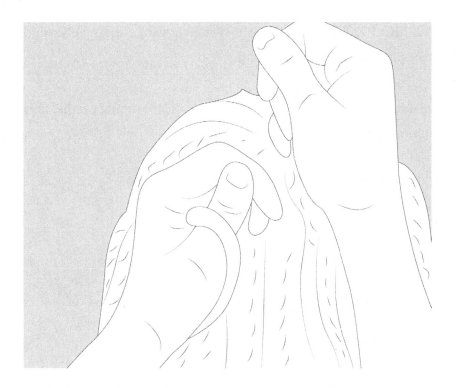

- 15th round: K2. K2tog. Repeat around. 24 sts.
- 17th round: K1. K2tog. Repeat around. 16 sts.
- 18th round: K2tog. Repeat around. 8 sts.
- Break yarn, leaving a long end. Thread end through remaining sts and draw up tightly. Fasten securely.

For the Pompom:

- Wrap A around four fingers approximately 90 times. Remaining over from fingers and tie tightly in the center. Cut through each side of the loops. Trim to a smooth round shape. Sew to the top of the Hat

2. Extra Warm Hat Knit

Materials:

- Yarn: Worsted, dk, or any yarn held together in two strands
- 10 1/2 circular needles and #10 or #10 1/2 dpn needles to finish the top of the hat

Gauge:

- 3 sts/inch. # 10 1/2 circular needles

Instructions:

- CO on 60 stitches, join, and begin knitting in the round. Work 8 inches, alternating a row of knitting and a row of purl for garter stitch.
- Row 1: (Knit 8, K 2 tog) repeat six times: 54 sts
- Row 2 and all even rows: Work even

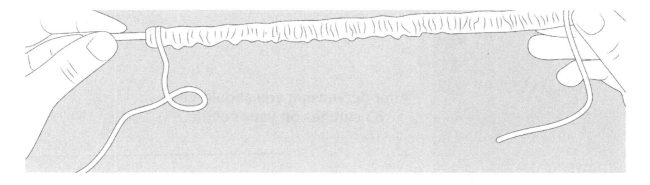

- Row 3: (Knit 7, k 2 tog) 6 times: 48 sts
- Row 5: (Knit 6, k 2 tog) 6 times: 42 sts

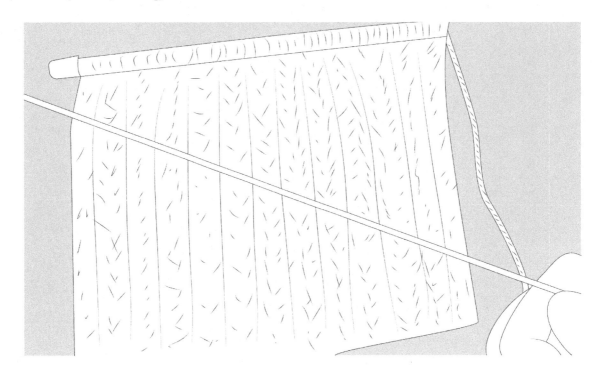

- Row 7: (Knit 5, K 2 tog) 6 times: 36 sts
- Row 9: (Knit 4, K 2 tog) 6 times: 30 sts
- Row 11: (Knit 3, K 2 tog) 6 times: 24 sts

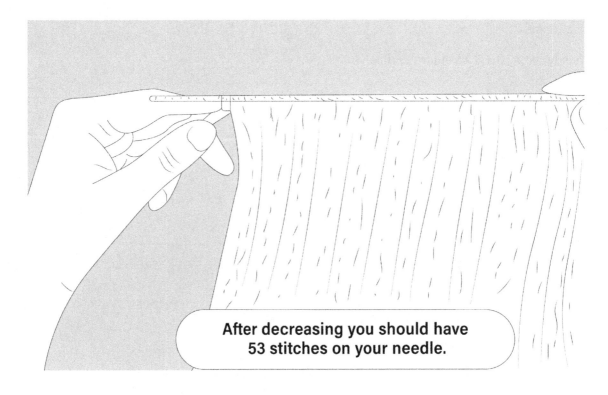

After decreasing you should have 53 stitches on your needle.

- Row 13: (Knit 2, K2 tog) 6 times: 18 sts
- Row 15: (Knit 1, K2 tog) 6 times: 12 sts
- Row 17: (K 2 tog) 6 times: 6 sts

- Row 18: Knit even
- Cut yarn, thread tail through remaining six sts, and pull. Bring the tail to the inside of the hat, and weave it in.

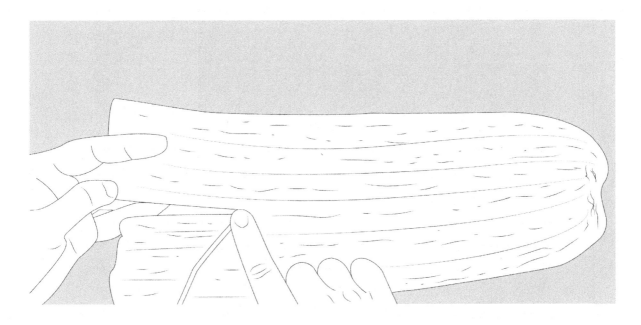

- Wear with the brim folded up.

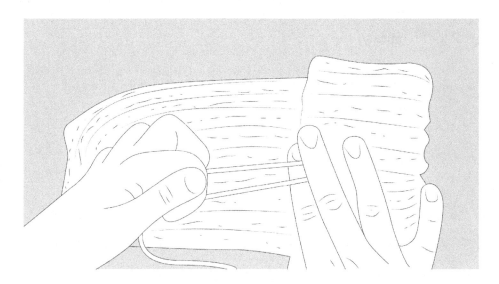

3. Christmas Knit Hat

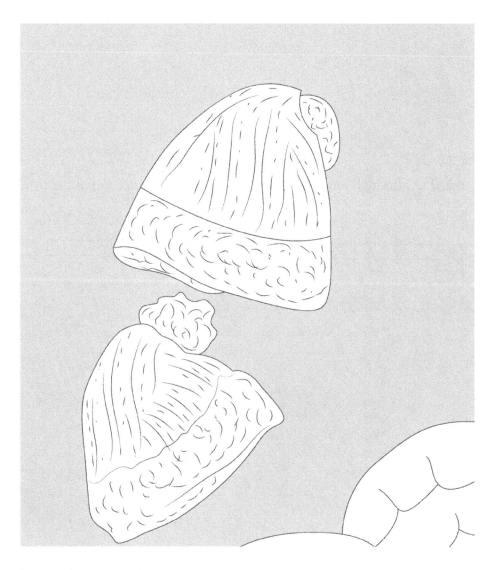

Materials:

- Size 6 US (4.25 mm) 16" circular needles
- Size 6 US (4.25 mm)double points
- One ball Splash (Color White #101) by Crystal Palace Yarns
- 100% polyester
- 94 yards/100 grams
- Two skeins of Cotton Chenille (Color Apple Red #8166) by Crystal Palace Yarns
- 100% mercerized cotton
- 98 yards/50 grams

Gauge:

- 16 sts=4" in St st with Cotton Chenille

Instructions:

- With Splash and circular needles, CO 70 (60) sts. Join, being careful not to twist. Place marker for beg of round.
- Knit with Splash for nine rounds.

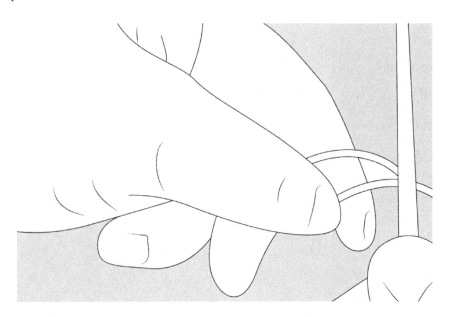

- Change to Cotton Chenille and knit in St st. For 7" for the crown of the hat.
- Begin dec rows as follows (when the diameter gets too small for circular needles, change to the double point needles).
- K8, k2tog; rep from
- Knit 8 (7) rounds
- K7, k2tog; rep from

- Knit 8(7) rounds
- K6, k2tog; rep from

- Knit 8 (7) rounds
- K5, k2tog; rep from
- Knit 8 (7) rounds
- K4, k2tog; rep from

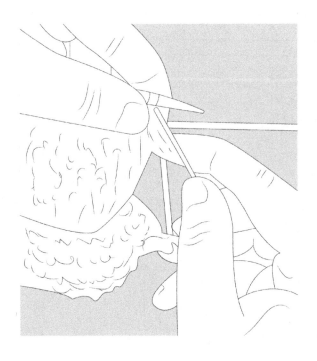

- Knit 4 (3) rounds
- K3, k2tog; rep from
- Knit 4 (3) rounds
- K2, k2tog; rep from

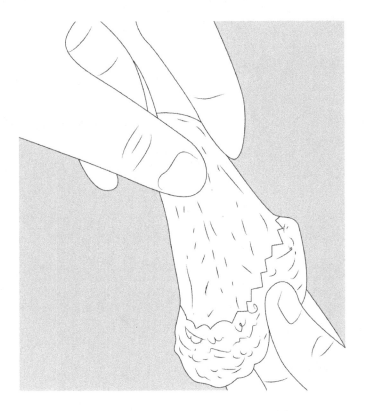

- Knit 4 (3) rounds
- K1, k2tog; rep from
- Knit 2 (2) rounds
- K2tog around until 1 st remain and fasten off.
- Make a Splash Pom-Pom and attach it.

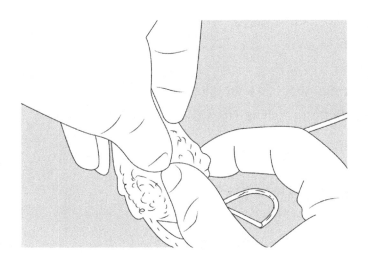

4. Hoodie Hat

Materials:

- Needles: US 17
- Yarn: 4, medium weight, about 50 total grams, four strands
- Extra: Yarn needle, fun yarn—about 10 yards

Gauge:

- 16 S in 4 inches, not required but advisable

Instructions:

- With the four strands, cast on 22 stitches.

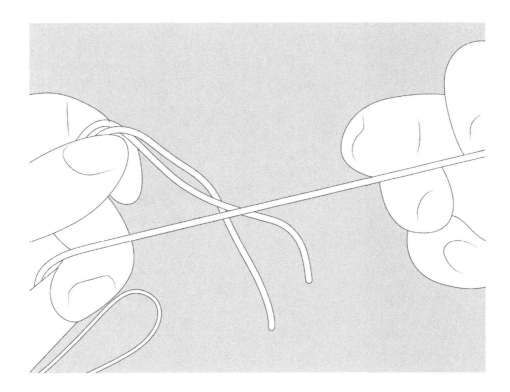

- Knit each row until you make a 24-inch wide rectangle.
- Cast off with 15 inches of a yarn tail.

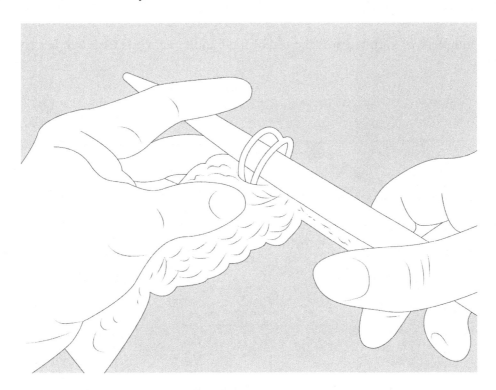

- Fold your rectangle in half and sew the back seam together with the yarn needle. Turn the hat right-side out so that the seam is on the inside.
- Add fun yarn to the two sides of the hat so that it hangs down by the ears in tassels and one long tassel at the top, if you want.

To Make a Tassel:

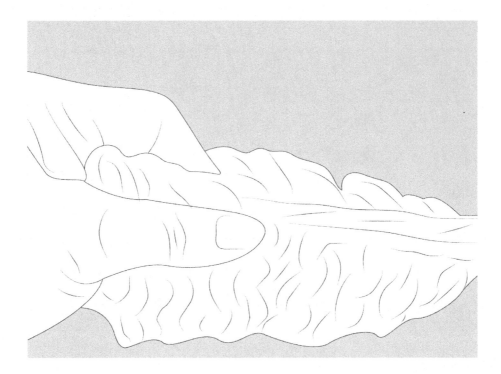

- With fun yarn, wrap it around your four fingers approximately 20 times. Tie securely through the loop.
- Tie a second piece of yarn towards the top of the bundle, which is tied together so small ball forms at the top.

- Trim the ends of the tassel so they are loose.
- Insert the ends of the tie holding the bundle together at the sides and on the top of your hat and tie securely on the inside. Intertwine the ends into the finished work.

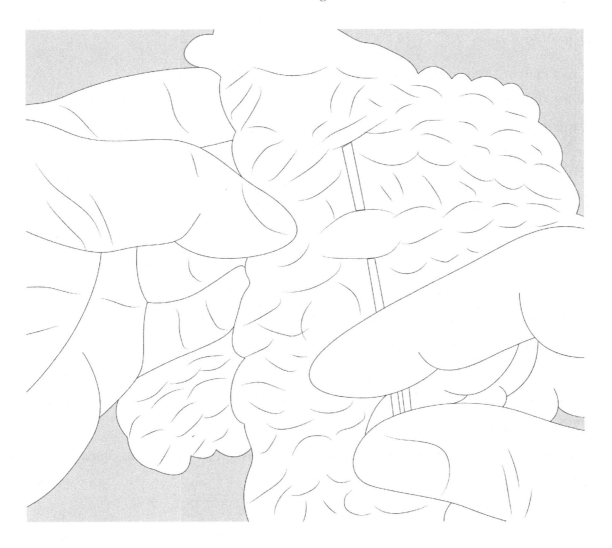

5. Frog Eye Hat Knit

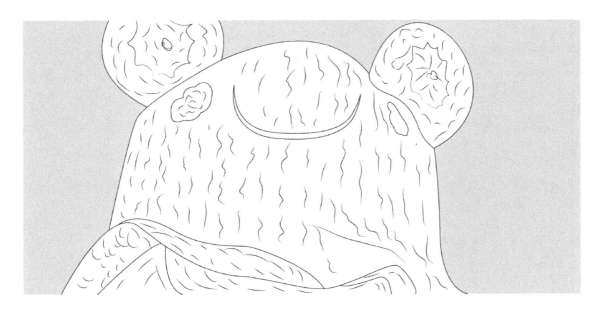

Materials:

- Size 5 dpns or size to get gauge
- Worsted-weight green yarn.
- Darning needle.

Gauge:

- Stitch gauge: 1 inch = 4.75 sts x 7 rows on size 5 needles
- 2×2 ribbing – k2, p2
- PCB3 – Purl Cable Back 3: slip one to the cable needle and hold it back. k2, then p1 from the cable needle
- PCF3 – Purl Cable Front 3: slip two cable needles, and hold to the front. p1, then k2 from the cable needle
- PCB4 – Purl Cable Back 4: Slip two sts to cable needle, hold to back, p2, k2 from cable needle
- PCF4 – Purl Cable Front 4: Slip two sts to cable needle, hold to front, p2, k2 from cable needle

Instructions:

- Using a longtail or another stretchy cast-on method, cast on 80 [88 96] sts. Spread stitches equally across four needles.

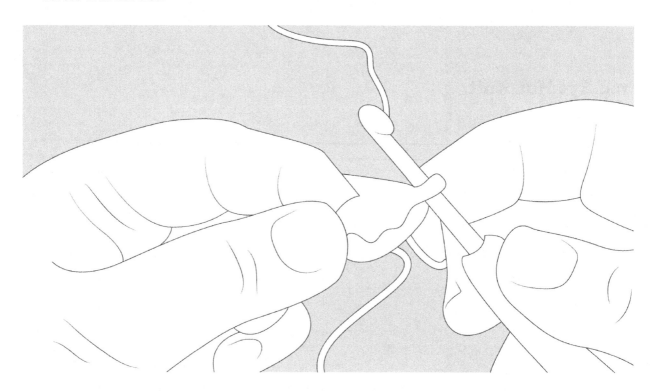

- Work 12 rows in a 2×2 rib.

For the Cable Pattern:

- On even rows, k in k sts, p in p sts. You do four repeats of the parenthesis.
- Rows 1 -4: (p4 [5 6], k2, p8 [9 10], k2, p4)
- Row 5: (p4 [5 6], k2, p7 [8 9], k4, p3)

- Row 7: (p4 [5 6], k2, p6 [7 8], PCB3, PCF3, p2)
- Row 9: (p4 [5 6], k2, p4 [5 6], PCB4, p2, PCF4)
- Row 11: (p4 [5 6], k2, p4 [5 6], k2, p6, k2)
- Row 13: (p4 [5 6], k2, p4 [5 6], PCF4, p2, PCB4)
- Row 15: (p4 [5 6], k2, p6 [7 8], PCF3, PCB3, p2)
- Row 17: (p4 [5 6], k2, p7 [8 9], k4, p3)
- Row 19: (p4 [5 6], k2, p8 [9 10], k2, p4)
- Row 21: (p3 [4 5], k4, p7 [8 9], k2, p4)
- Row 23: (p2 [3 4], PCB3, PCF3, p6 [7 8], k2, p4)
- Row 25: (p0 [1 2], PCB4, p2, PCF4, p4 [5 6], k2, p4)
- Row 27: (p0 [1 2], k2, p6, k2, p4 [5 6], k2, p4)

- Row 29: (p0 [1 2], PCF4, p2, PCB4, p4 [5 6], k2, p4)
- Row 31: (p2 [3 4], PCF3, PCB3, p6 [7 8], k2, p4)
- Row 33: (p3 [4 5], k4, p7 [8 9], k2, p4)
- Row 35: (p4 [5 6], k2, p8 [9 10], k2, p4)

For the Crown:

- To do the crown, you'll want to shift your needle placements. To do so, p4,k1. This is the new start of the round. Four repeats of the parenthesis.
- Row 1: (k1, p7 [8 9], k4, p7 [8 9], k1)
- Row 3: (ssk, p5 [6 7], PCB3, PCF3, p5 [6 7], k2tog)
- Row 5: (ssk, p3 [4 5], PCB4, p2, PCF4, p3 [4 5], k2tog)
- Row 7: (ssk, p1 [2 3], k2, p6, k2, p1 [2 3], k2tog)

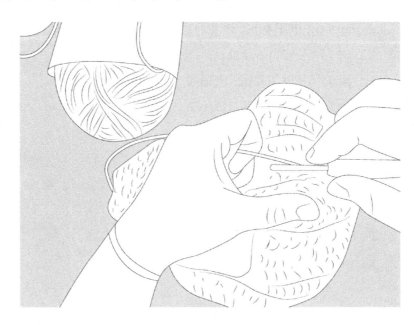

- Row 9: (ssk, p0 [1 2], PCF4, p2, PCB4, p0 [1 2], k2tog)
- Row 11: (ssk, p1 [2 3], PCF3, PCB3, p1 [2 3], k2tog)
- Row 13: (ssk, p1 [2 3], k4, p1 [2 3], k2tog)

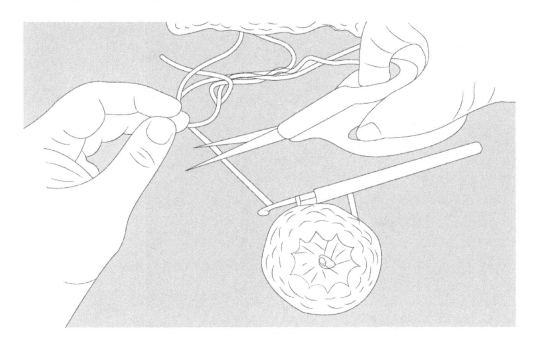

- Row 15: (ssk, p1 [2 3], k2, p1 [2 3], k2tog)
- Row 17: (ssk, k0 [1 2], k2, k0 [1 2], k2tog)
- Row 19: (ssk, k0 [1 ssk], k2tog)

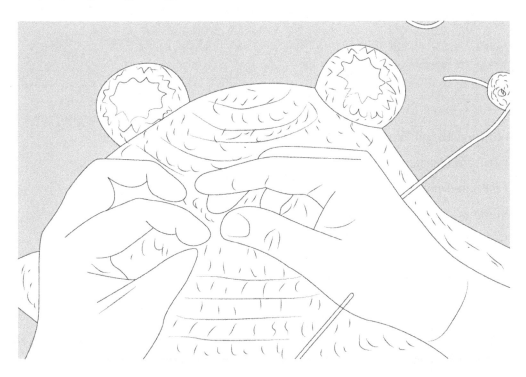

- Pull yarn through the remaining stitches. Weave in ends. Finish the hat with a pom-pom.

6. Ribbed Cabled Knit Hat

Materials:

- 1 skein of Lion Brand Wool-Ease Chunky or any other bulky weight yarn
- 1 set of 16" circular needles in size 10 ½
- 1 set of 5 double-pointed needles in size 10 ½
- Stitch Markers
- Cable Needle
- Yarn Needle

Instructions:

- Using your circular needles and a longtail cast-on, CO 72 stitches and join to knit in the round.
- K1, P1 Repeat to end of first round and PM.

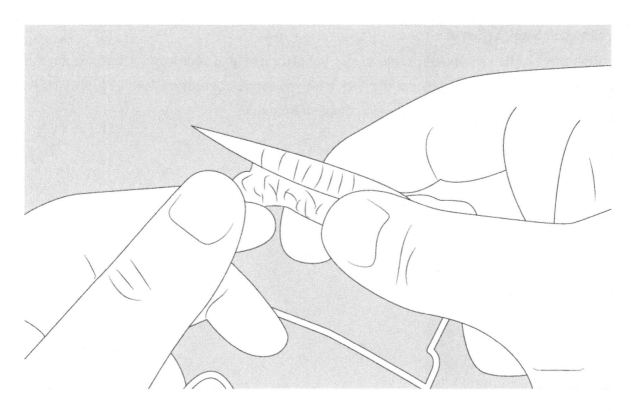

- Continue in K1 and P1 ribbing until your piece measures four inches long.
- Round 1: P2, K6 (for cable), P2, K2, P1, K2, P1, K2, PM
- Repeat this pattern three more times, placing a second marker at the beginning of your second round, so you know where the next round begins.

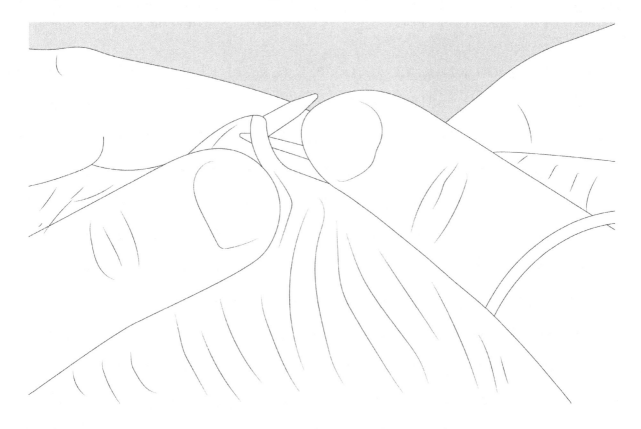

- Round 2: Same as Round 1.
- Round 3: P2, SL 3 sts onto the cable needle and place it behind your work. K the next three sts, then K the three sts from the cable needle back onto your circular needle. P2, K2, P1, K2, P1, K2, SM. Repeat this pattern three more times to complete Round 3.

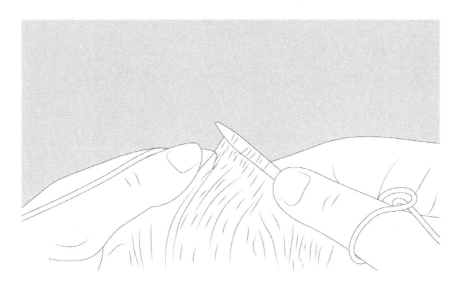

- Repeat Round 1 for five rounds, repeating round 3 in the next round.
- Continue this pattern until your hat measures 8".
- To begin decreasing, P2, K2, K2TOG, K2, P2, K2TOG, P1, K2TOG, P1, K2TOG, SM.
- Continue the pattern three more times for the rest of this round.
- Onto a DPN, P2, K5, P2, K1, P1, K1, P1, K1.Continue the pattern to the end of the round, so you have 14 sts each on 4 DPNs.
- Next Round: P2TOG, K2TOG, K1, K2TOG, P2TOG, K1, P1, K1, P1, K1. Repeat this pattern three more times until ten sts are on each needle.

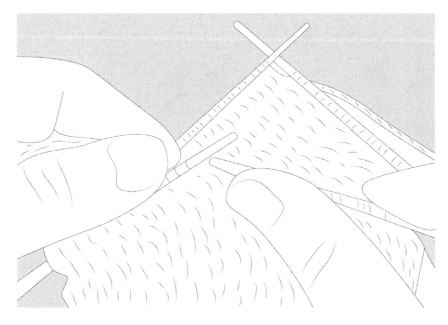

- P1, K3, P1, K1, P1, K1, P1, K1, repeating this pattern for the rest of the round.
- K2TOG for the entire round, leaving five sts on each of the 4 DPNs.
- K2TOG for another round, slipping the last st on Needles 1 and 3 to the next needle and leaving ten stitches. Cut the yarn, leaving 6-8 inches, and thread it through a yarn needle. Slip the sts off the DPNs and onto the yarn needle, running the yarn needle through the last ten sts and pulling it tight. Weave in all the ends and fold up the brim.

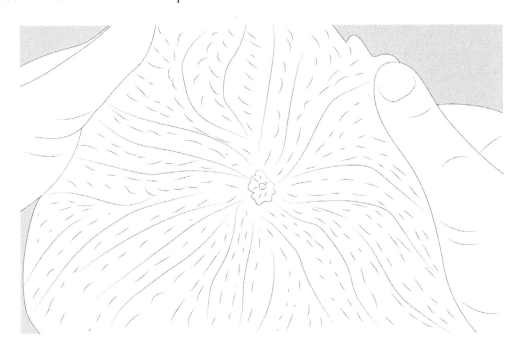

7. Blue Beret Hat

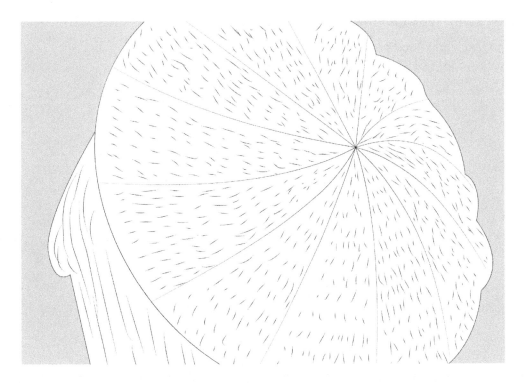

Materials:

- 1 ball of Lion Wool
- 4 & 8 DPNS

Gauge:

- (taken in the round, in the pattern) body=4st/inch
- ribbing=5st/inch un-stretched

Instructions:

- Cast on 72 with size four needles

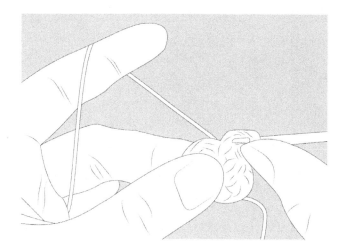

- Work k1p1 around for 1.5 inches
- Next row, k2m1, repeat for row
- Switch to size eight needles

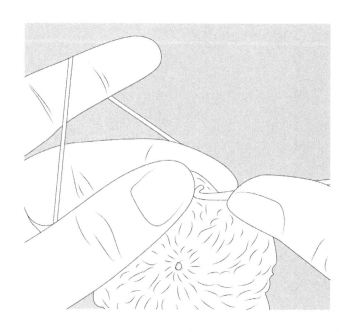

- K8p1 repeat for row

- Work till the full length of the hat is: 8.5 inches for tam; 7 inches for the toque

- K2 together four times, p1 repeat for row

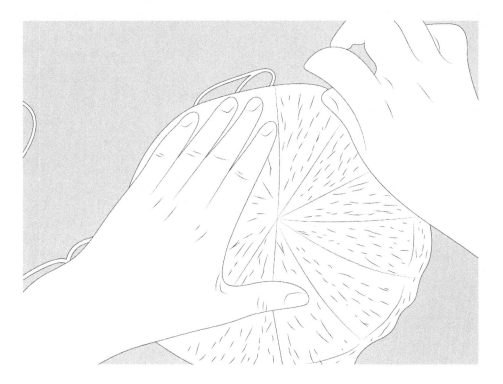

- K2 together two times, p1 repeat for row

- K2 together, p1 repeat for row

- Cut a long tail, and thread it through the remaining stitches three times, weave the end inside the hat

- Weave in the cast on the tail.

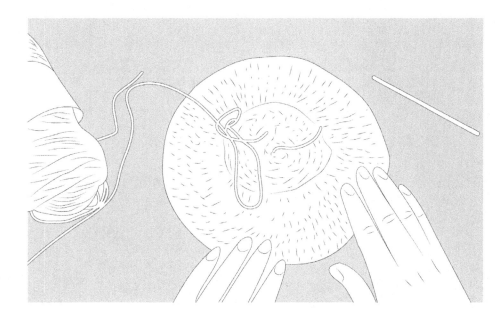

- For the toque, make a two-inch pompom, trim, and fasten.

8. Flower Baby Hat

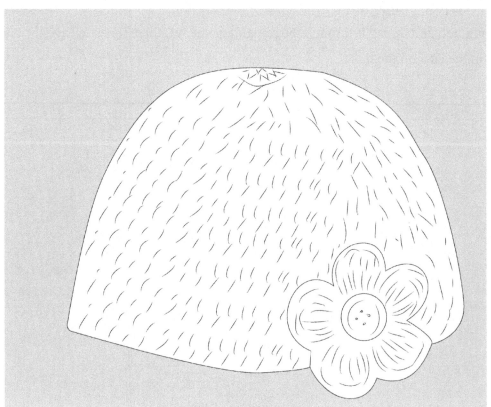

Materials:

- 80 Yards Of Worsted Weight Yarn (#4)
- 8 Yards Of DK Or Worsted For Flower
- 4 Yards Of DK Or Worsted For Leaves
- Size 7 Double-Pointed Needles

Gauge:

- 5 Stitches = 1 Inch On Size 7

Instructions:

Instructions are given for newborns, with 3-6 months and 6-12 months in parentheses.

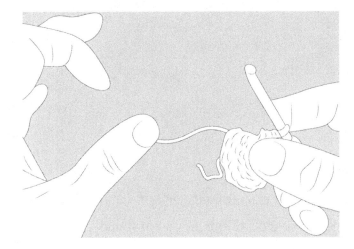

- Cast on 60 (70, 80) stitches. Knit around and attach yarn to the beginning stitch to close the gap.
- Continue knitting every round until the piece measures 5.5" (6.5", 7.5"). NOTE: If you want the brim to roll more, keep knitting for another inch.

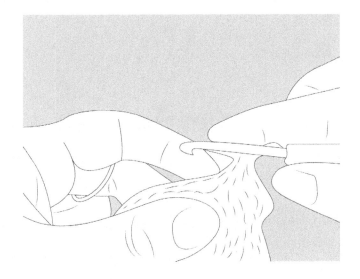

To work the crown, do the decrease rows as follows: -Round 1: Knit 8 st, K2TOG; repeat from to end of round—54 (63, 72) sts remaining.

- Round 2 and all even-numbered rounds: K.
- Round 3: Knit 7 st, K2TOG; repeat from the end of round—48 (56, 64) sts remaining.
- Round 5: Knit 6 st, K2TOG; repeat from the end of round—42 (49, 56) sts remaining.
- Round 7: Knit 5 st, K2TOG; repeat from the end of round—36 (42, 48) sts remaining.
- Round 9: Knit 4 st, K2TOG; repeat from the end of round—30 (35, 40) sts remaining.

- Round 11: Knit 3 st, K2TOG; repeat from the end of round—24 (28, 32) sts remaining.
- Round 13: Knit 2 st, K2TOG; repeat from the end of round—18 (21, 24) sts remaining.
- Round 15: Knit 1 st, K2TOG; repeat from the end of round—12 (14, 16) sts remaining.
- Round 17: K2TOG; repeat from the end of round—6 (7, 8) sts remaining.

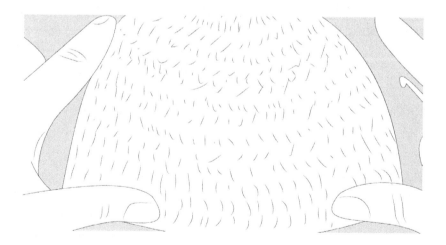

- After Round 17, cut yarn, leaving a 6-inch tail. Thread the tail onto a darning needle and then weave the needle through the remaining stitches. Slide them off the needles and pull like a drawstring to close the hole. Weave in the remainder of the tail.

For the Rose:

The rose is worked in one long strip and then rolled up. You'll start by making four small petals, then three medium-sized petals, and three large petals, and they are all connected. It looks like many instructions, but this easy knitting works very fast.

- Cast on 5 st.
- Row 1: K1 f&b, K4—6 sts total.
- Row 2: P4, P1 f&b, P1—7 sts total.
- Row 3: K7.
- Row 4: P7.
- Row 5: K1, K2tog, K4—6 sts.
- Row 6: P3, P2tog, P1—5 sts total.
- Repeat Rows 1-6 three more times, so you'll end with four petals.

Now, you will proceed to knit the medium petals on the same strip, so don't cut your yarn; just keep knitting.

- Row 7: K1 f&b, K4—6 sts total.
- Row 8: P4, P1 f&b, P1—7 sts total.
- Row 9: K1 f&b, K6—8 sts total.
- Row 10: P6, P1 f&b, P1—9 sts total.
- Rows 11 and 13: K9.

- Rows 12 and 14: P9.
- Rows 15 and 17: K1, K2tog, K to end.
- Rows 16 and 18: P to last three sts; P2tog, P1. You should have five sts remaining at the end of Row 18.
- Repeats Rows 7-18 two more times so you've added three petals to the strip.
- Next, knit the large petals on the same strip without cutting your yarn.
- Rows 19, 21, and 23: K1 f&b, K to end.
- Rows 20, 22, and 24: P to last two sts; P1 f&b, P1. At the end of Row 24, you should have 11 sts.
- Rows 25, 27 and 29: K11.
- Rows 26, 28 and 30: P11.
- Rows 31, 33, and 35: K1, K2tog, K to end.
- Rows 32, 34, and 36: P to last three sts; P2tog, P1. At the end of Row 36, you should have five sts.
- Repeat Rows 19-36 two more times.
- Row 37: K1, K2tog, K2—4 sts remaining.
- Row 38: P1, P2tog, P1—3 sts.
- Row 39: K1, K2tog—2 sts.
- Row 40: P2tog. Cut the tail and slip through the last stitch. Tighten the strand to secure the knot.
- Press the petal strip. Starting from the small petal end, roll up the strip with the WRONG side facing outwards. Stitch the bottom edges together, so your rose does not unwind. Curl the petals outward.

For the Leaf:

You will make two leaves—a small and a big one.

- For the large leaf, cast on 3 st.
- Row 1 and all odd-numbered (Wrong Side) rows: P.
- Row 2 (RS): [K1 f&b] twice, K1—5 sts total.
- Row 4: [K1 f&b] twice, K3—7 sts total.
- Row 6: [K1 f&b] twice, K5—9 sts total.
- Row 8: [K1 f&b] twice, K7—11 sts total.
- Row 10: [K1 f&b] twice, K9—13 sts total.
- Row 12: K.
- Row 14: SSK, K9, K2tog—11 sts total.
- Row 16: SSK, K7, K2tog—9 sts total.
- Row 18: SSK, K5, K2tog—7 sts total.
- Row 20: SSK, K3, K2tog—5 sts total.
- Row 22: SSK, K1, K2tog—3 sts total.
- Row 24: Sl2, PSSO—1 st.
- Cut the tail and slip through the last stitch. Tighten the strand to secure the knot.
- For the small leaf, follow the same pattern for Rows 1-7, OMIT Rows 8-15, and finish with Rows 16-24.

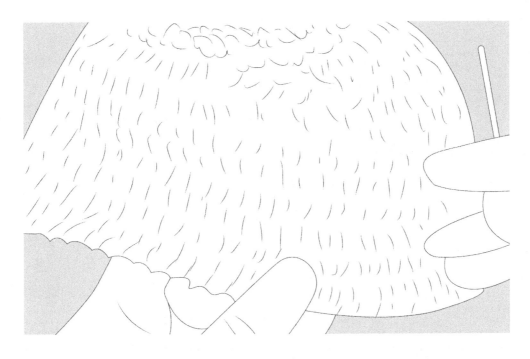

- Attach one tip of each leaf to the stitched base of the flower. Before attaching the flower to the hat, roll up the brim so it is placed where it will be seen and not inside the brim!

PART 3

KNITTING COLORFUL VESTS

CHAPTER 1:
GAUGE AND TECHNIQUES

Gauge

The best way to ensure the piece you are knitting will size up with the pattern you have chosen is to knit a sample swatch. Do you knit tightly or loosely? Is the yarn you have chosen different from the one specified in the pattern? Many factors contribute to your knitting gauge, so it just makes sense to knit up a small swatch (4" x 4") to double-check. Every pattern will provide a gauge; this number shows how the pattern's stitch count was calculated, given in stitches and rows per inch.

Start by looking at your pattern. What's the gauge? Compare this measurement to the one on the yarn label. Choose a yarn with the same gauge as your pattern (or very close). You can adjust the swatch by changing

116

the needle size, bigger or smaller, but you need to understand that using a larger needle than recommended will create a loose knit that might look like it has holes. On the opposite end of this spectrum, a smaller needle size produces a denser, tighter fabric with less give.

The best way to ensure you get the right width is to knit a small sample. I like to use 12 stitches for my samples because it breaks down into easy multiples: half = ten stitches; one-fourth = 4 stitches; quarter = 3 stitches. You need to know how many stitches per inch to multiply that number by the number of inches you want.

For example, you knit a sample using 12 stitches, and the width of your finished sample is 3 inches. That means you knit this yarn on these needles at a gauge of 4 stitches per inch. If you want a hat that measures 20 inches, you need to work 80 stitches (20 inches X 4 stitches/inch).

Techniques

Chain Cast Off

This basic cast-off stitch is the most widely accepted by beginners to bind their projects off. You first knit two stitches from the left to the right needle to do this stitch. Now, you have two stitches on the right needle. Then, using the edge of the left needle, drive the first stitch of the right needle over the second one and drop it off. Repeat the process until you have no stitches on the left needle, only on the right one. After cutting the working yarn, pull the yarn out through the remaining stitches, and you have finally secured your knitted project from raveling. If you would like, you can use the purl stitch instead of the knit stitch.

Looser Bind Off

One complaint we always hear from knitters is that the basic bind-off is too tight and uncomfortable to use. Not to worry, we have a solution for this issue in the form of the looser bind-off technique. Knit two stitches together from the left needle to get a stitch on the right, then slide the newly knitted stitch onto the left needle. Repeat the process, merging the new stitch with a stitch from the left needle, and continue with this until you have only one stitch left on the right needle, then follow the finishing steps as you would for the basic cast-off.

Unraveling

Though we have many options to fix our mistakes, sometimes the work is more time-consuming than simply unraveling the stitches until you reach the mistake. Though this sounds horrifying, it can be the best option. So, stop worrying about the best way to repair the mistake, unravel and begin again.

Sew It Up

Sometimes we notice unusual and unwanted holes in our project, which can be scary and become a nightmare if we try to meet a deadline. Unraveling at this point may not be an option because of time restraints. An easy fix is to sew those holes closed with matching yarn, and your work is done. Those holes can barely be seen outside, and you will have your perfectly shaped product.

Flat Knitting

Flat knitting is the process of knitting in rows, where you periodically turn the work. There is a 'right side' and a 'wrong side' of the project. Once you have Cast On, you immediately knit the next row from the pattern.

Here is a guide to starting flat knitting:

- Step 1: Place your right needle behind the left needle.
- Step 2: Wrap the yarn counterclockwise around the right needle and behind the left needle.
- Step 3: Pull the yarn through the loop so it is on the right needle (like above).
- Step 4: Here's where it gets different. Push the first stitch on the left needle off of the needle completely.
- Step 5: You'll have fewer stitches on the left needle and one on the right.
- Step 6: Continue this same method down the row.
- Step 7: Once all the stitches are off the left needle and on the right needle, that row is done.
- Step 8: For the next row, move what was your right needle to your left hand now and your left needle to your right hand (flip them). The needle with the stitches on it will always start in your left hand.
- Step 9: Continue stitching the next row as you did the first.
- Step 10: When the next row is done, you will begin to see the pattern forming.

Circular Knitting

Circular knitting – or in the round – is a form of knitting that creates a seamless tube. The yarn is cast using circular knitting needles, and the circle of stitches is joined. This type of knitting is perfect for creating socks, mittens, or bigger projects like sweaters.

Here is a step-by-step guide for this type of knitting:

If you don't join the ends, you can use your circular needle to knit flat pieces as you'd knit on conventional needles. Because of the long connector between the needles, you can knit large items like afghans and not have to join them.

You can also knit in the round on your circular needles. When you do, you'll find that the right side of the work is facing toward you, making patterns easy to see.

You cast onto your circular needle the same way you cast onto straight needles.

Continue to cast until you have the number of stitches required for your pattern. You'll find that the circular needle is now full.

It is crucial when joining your work that it is not twisted around the needle! If your piece is twisted, you will have to rip it out. Hold your needle, so the yarn is coming from the right to join. When knitting in the round, it is a good idea to use a stitch marker to know where your piece began - slip one onto your needle now if you will be using one. Place your knitting on a flat surface and carefully turn your cast-on stitches so that they are all facing in the same way (in our example, they are facing to the bottom and inside of the needle.)

Then insert the right needle into the first stitch you cast on and knit the stitch. Be sure to pull the first stitches tight so you don't get a gap where the rounds join.

Continue to knit – you'll find that the 'right' side is always on the outside and that, as your work grows, patterns are easy to see!

Around Neck

1. With the stated side facing and working from right to left, insert the right-hand needle through the horizontal loop of the first required cast-on stitch (L).
2. Wrap the yarn around the needle and pull through as if to knit (M).
3. Insert the right-hand needle up through the horizontal loop of the next cast-on stitch (N).
4. Repeat steps 2 and 3 until the required number of stitches have been worked.

Making I-Cord

Worked on two double-pointed needles.

1. Cast on the number of stitches needed using Long Tail Cast-On (A).
2. Without turning your work, slide the stitches to the right-hand end of the needle (B).
3. Bringing the working yarn around the back (C), knit the first stitch, pull the yarn tight, and knit to the end of the row.
4. Repeat steps 2 and 3 until the required length is reached, tugging on the cast-on tail after every row to form a tube (D).
5. To cast off, cut the yarn and thread the tail end onto a tapestry needle; carefully slide stitches off the knitting needle and, working from right to left, push the tapestry needle with yarn tail through the stitches and draw up (E and F).

Joining New Yarn Balls

It may sound funny that you need to know how to join new yarn to the yarn you started the project with. You cannot join the yarns by tying a knot. This will cause a bumpy knot on your beautifully knitted product. Then, what to do? There is a solution to this problem also. Combine the new and old yarn, wrap the needle around it, and continue knitting. After creating two to three stitches drop the old yarn and continue with the new yarn. Tie both ends together to keep them safe.

Seaming

This is the ultimate stage where your favorite knitted product will get its final shape. Seaming is a step that cannot be avoided, whether you want a scarf, a sweater, or gloves. You should maintain even tension while seaming, and if you have long tails in your cast-on row, you can use those for seaming with a yarn needle.

Different stitches are available here, like a mattress stitch, invisible horizontal stitch, backstitch, overcasting stitch, and more. Whatever pattern you choose, the ultimate target of sewing the end is to give the final product its finest form. The easiest way to seam is to lay down the knit pattern, keeping the inside out, and sew the edges, making sure to match the ends properly.

CHAPTER 2:
PATTERNS AND PROJECTS

1. Simple Vest Knitting Pattern

Materials:

- Needles: US 10.5 or 6.5 mm
- Yarn: 5 bulky, four balls or skeins
- Extra: 2 stitch holders, yarn needle

Gauge and Size:

- Gauge: 14 S X 18 R in 4 inches using a stocking stitch
- Size: 28 inches

Instructions:

For the Right Front:

- With No. 4 needles cast on 46(50) sts. Work in ribbing and moss st border as follows: Row 1: K1, p1, repeat from across to last two sts, k2

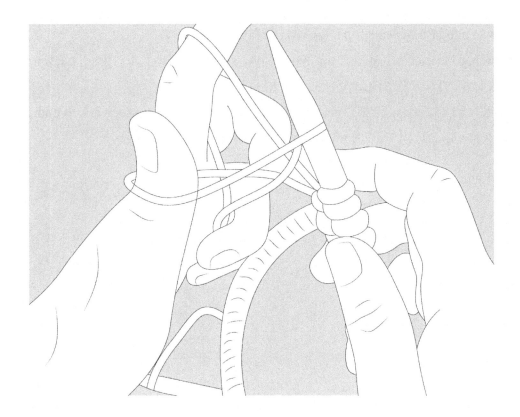

- Row 2: K1, p1, repeat from across to last six sts, k2, (p1, k1) twice.
- Row 3: (buttonhole row): K1, k2 tog, yo, (p1, k1) 12(14) times, yo, k2 tog, work ribbing to last st, k1
- Row 4: Repeat row 2. Repeat rows 1 through 4 once more, then rows 1 through 3.
- Next Row: (Work ribbing on next ten sts, inc in next st) 3(2) times, work ribbing to end – 49 (52) sts. Changes to larger needles and work next six rows for pat st and moss st borders as follows: Row 1: (K1, p1) twice, k1, p3, k1, yo, sl one as if to k, k1, psso, p3, k to end.

- Row 2: K1, p to last 14 sts, k3, p3, k4, (p1, k1) twice.
- Row 3: (K1, p1) twice, k1, p2, k2 tog, yo, k1, yo, sl one as if to k, k1, psso, p2, k to end.
- Row 4: K1, p to last 14 sts, k2, p5, k3, (p1, k1) twice.
- Row 5: (K1, p1) 3 times, k2 tog, yo, k3, yo, sl one as if to k, k1, psso, p1, k to end.
- Row: 6: K1, p to last 14 sts, k1, p7, k2, (p1, k1) twice.

To Shape Front Edge:

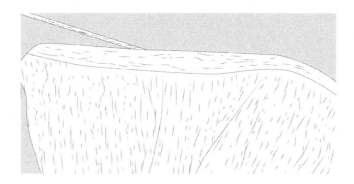

- First Dec Row: (K1, p1) twice, k1, p3, k1, yo, sl one as to k, k1, psso, p3, k1, k2 tog through the back loop (tb1), k to end.
- Next Row: Work Row 2 of pat st. Keeping to pat, dec 1 st in the same manner as the first dec row inside the lace panel on the next row, then every other row until 37(40) sts remain, end right side.

To Shape Armhole and Front Slope:

- Bind off 5(6) sts, work to end, Keeping to pat, dec 1 st at armhole edge on next five rows, then on every other row, AND AT THE SAME TIME, dec 1 st inside lace panel on 3rd, then every 4th row until 23 sts remain. Keeping armhole edge straight, continue to dec inside lace panel every 4th row from the previous dec until 16(17) sts remain. Work until the piece measures 9-1/2 (10)" from beg, end at the armhole edge.

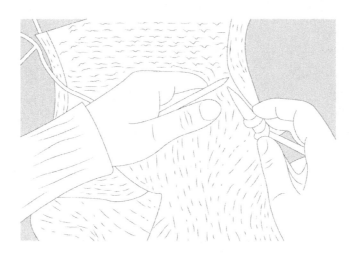

To Shape Shoulder:

- Bind off six sts at the beg of the next row. Work 1 row even. Bine off 5(6) sts at the beg of the next row. Work even in moss st on the remaining five sts for 1-1/2" until stretched. Bind off in moss st.

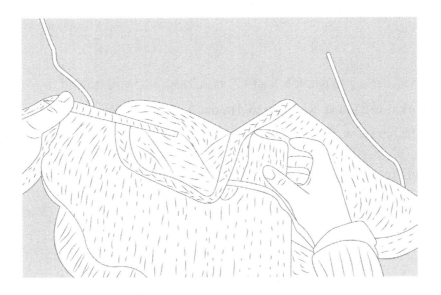

For the Left Front:

- With No. 4 needles, cast on 46(50) sts. Work in ribbing and moss st border: Row 1: K2, p1, k1 repeat from across.
- Row 2: (K1, p1) twice, k2, p1, k1, repeat from across. Repeat Rows 1 and 2 four times more, then Row 1 again.
- Next Row: Work in ribbing on first 13(28) sts, (inc in next st, working ribbing on next ten sts) 2(3) times – 49 (52) sts. Change to No. 6 needles and work next six rows for pat st and moss st borders as follows: Row 1: K to last 14 sts, p3, k1, yo, sl one as if to k, k1, psso, p3 (k1, p1) twice, k1.
- Row 2: (K1, p1) twice, k4, p3, k3, p to last st, k1.

- Row 3: K to last 14 ss, p2, k2 tog, yo, k1, yo, sl one as if to k, k1, psso, p2, (k1, p1) twice, k1.
- Row 4: (K1, p1) twice, k3, p5, k2, p to last st, k1.
- Row 5: K to last 14 sts, p1, k2 tog, yo, k3, yo, sl1 as if to k, k1, psso (p1, k1) 3 times.
- Row 6: (K1, p1) twice, k2, p7, k1, p to last st, k1.

To Shape Front Slope:

- First DEC Row: Keeping to pat, k to last 17 sts, k2 tog, k1, work to end.
- Next Row: Work row 2 pat st. Keeping to pat, dec 1 st in the same manner as the first dec row inside lace panel on the next row, then every other row until 38(41) sts remain, end on the wrong side.

To Shape Armhole and Front Slope:

- Bind of 5(6) sts, work last 17 sts, k2 tog, k1, work to end, Work 1 row. Complete to correspond to right front, reversing shapings.

For the Back:

- With No. 4 needles, cast on 63(69) sts. Work even in ribbing: Row 1: K2, p1, k1, repeat from across to las st, k1.
- Row 2: K1, p1, repeat from across to last st, k1. Repeat rows 1 and 2 four times more, then row 1 again.
- Next Row: Work ribbing on first 1(4) sts, (inc in next st, work ribbing on next 19 sts) 3 times, inc in next st, work in ribbing to end-67(73) sts. Change to No. 6 needles and work 28 rows, even in St st.

To Shape Armholes:

- Bind off 5(6) sts at the beg of the next two rows. Dec 1 st at beg of the next two rows. Dec 1 st at each edge of the next five rows, then every other row until 43(45) sts remain. Work even in St st. Until the piece measures the same as front to beg of shoulder shaping, end p row.

To Shape Shoulders:

- Bind off six sts at the beg of the next two rows, then 5(6) sts at the beg of the next two rows. Bind off remaining 21 sts.

Finishing:

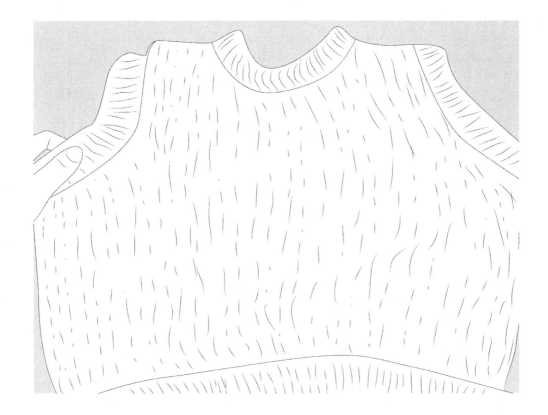

For the Armbands:

- Sew shoulder seams. With right side facing and smaller needles, pick up 76(84) sts along the armhole edge. Work in k1, p1 ribbing for 5 rows. Bind off in ribbing. Work another armband in the same manner. Sew side and armband seams. Sew ends of moss st; border tog, then sew edge to the back of the neck. Sew on buttons.

2. Rib-Line Vest

Materials.

8 (8, 9, 10) (12, 12, 14, 15) skeins of's Cashmere Tend, 100% cashmere. Each skein is about 82 backyards/ 50 grams; roughly 590 (650, 740, 810) (920, 985, 1075, 1165) lawns needed. We utilized the shade of Ice Gray.

The United States 7, 16-inch circular needles.

The United States 7, 24-inch circular needles.

The United States 7, 32-or 40-inch round needles (depending on the dimension you are making).

Sew pens consist of one distinct stitch or scrap yarn.

Instructions

Eighteen stitches and 28 rows = 4 inches in stockinette stitch.

19 stitches and 26 rows are = 4 inches in half-twisted rib stitch.

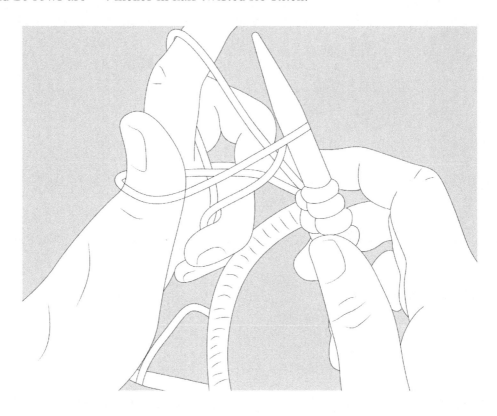

Sizes.

37 (40 1/2, 44, 47 1/2)(51 1/4, 54 3/4, 58 1/4, 61 3/4). To fit actual upper body circumference of 31-- 34 (34-- 37, 38-- 41, 41-- 44) (45-- 48, 49-- 52, 52-- 55, 56-- 59) inches, with roughly 3-- 6 inches of ease.

Finished Chest Circumference: 37 (40 1/2, 44, 47 1/2) (51 1/4, 54 3/4, 58 1/4,

61 3/4) inches. Polished Length from Shoulder To Bottom Edge: 20 3/4(21, 22 1/4, 22 3/4) (24 1/4, 24 1/2, 251/4, 26) inches. 7.

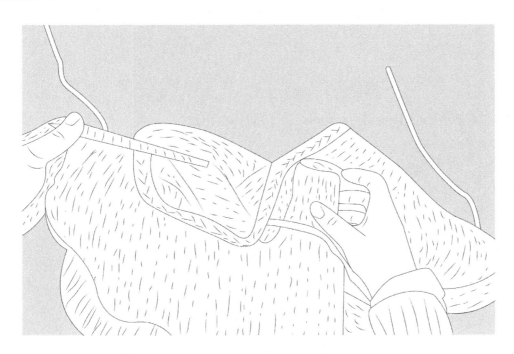

3. Silken Straw Summer Vest

Materials:

- Four skeins (for both dimensions) of Alchemy's Silken Straw, 100% Silk. This color is "Cornflower Blue."
- A 24-inch, US # 4 circular needle.
- 2 United States # 4 dual pointed needles.
- A stitch pen.

Assess:

- Unlocked: 6 1/2 stitches = 1 inch into stockinette..
- Obstructed: 6 stitches = 1 inch in stockinette.

Dimensions:

- Small/Medium (Medium/Large)
- Hip Circumference: 38 (42) inches.
- Upper body Circumference: 36 1/2 (40 1/2) inches.
- Size from Underarm to Bottom Edge: 18 inches.

NOTE: To amend the sizing, the most useful thing is to modify the gauge. Silken Straw is exceptionally responsive to evaluate variations! Split the actors on the number by your stitch-per-inch number, and also, you'll recognize the hip measurement. If you're knitting at 5 1/2 blocked stitches to the inch and also you adhere to the Medium/Large pattern, you'll end up with 45 3/4 inch hips (252 divided by 5.5 = 45.8

Instructions:

For the Body:

- With the 24-inch round needle, cast on 228 (252) stitches

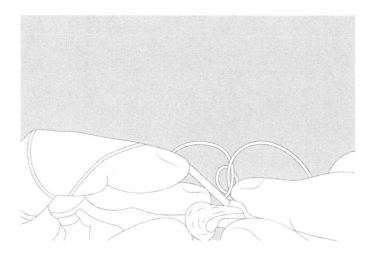

- Area a marker and join for operating in the round, taking care not to twist the stitches.
- Knit every round till the piece gauges 5 1/2 inches from the bottom side (unroll the edge to measure).
- Following round: K 114 (126), location pen, knit to end of the series.
- Decrease Round 1: Knit to last three stitches, SSK, k1. (1 stitch lowered).
- Minimize Round 2: K1, k2tog, knit to 3 stitches before the first pen, ssk, k1, slip pen, k1, k2tog, knit to finish the round. (3 stitches reduced).
- Knit 7 rounds. **.

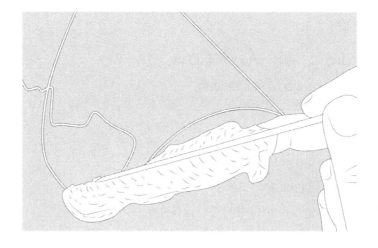

- Repeat from to * four more times. 208 (232) stitches

- Knit 14 rounds.

- Increase Round 1: Knit to last sew, make one right (m1r), k1. (1 stitch raised).

- Rise Round 2: K1, make one left (m1l), knit to 1 stitch before the initial pen, m1r, k1, slide marker, k1, m1l, knit to finish the round. (3 stitches raised).

- Knit 7 rounds. **.

- Repeat from to * two even more times, finishing the last round with six stitches before the completion marker. 220 (244) stitches.

For the Underarms:

- Bind off 12 stitches (eliminating pen), knit to 7 stitches before following a pen, bind off 12 stitches (removing pen), and knit 98 (110) stitches to the very first bind-off. 196 (220) stitches.

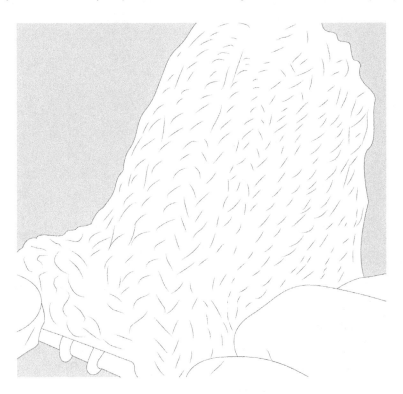

Cast on for Sleeves:

- Position a brand-new beginning-of-round pen; transform so the wrong side of the job is facing you and make use of a wired cast on to cast on 60 (65) stitches; turn so the best part of the work is encountering you, as well as, ensuring the cast on untwisted, knit the next 98 (110) stitches (to the following set of binding off underarm stitches); with the incorrect side encountering you, use a cable cast on cast on 60 (65) stitches; with the best surface faced, as well as, once more seeing to it the cast on isn't turned, for the Medium/Large dimension knit to the end; OR for the Small/Medium Size, knit to the last two stitches, k2tog. 315 (350) stitches.

For the Yoke:

- Knit till the sleeve gauges 2 inches from the wire cast on the side.
- Decrease Round: K3, k2tog, repeat to finish the round. 252 (280) stitches.
- Weave up until the sleeve measures 4 inches from the cord cast on the side.
- Decline Round: K2, k2tog, repeat to finish the round. 189 (210) stitches.
- Knit till the sleeve gauges 5 inches from the cable cast on the side.

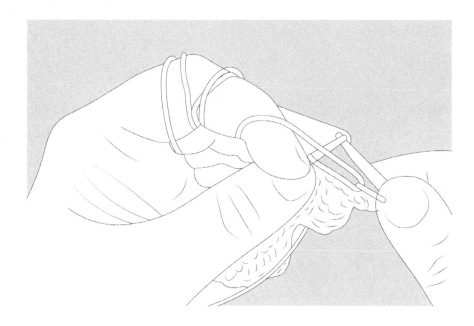

Framing Neckline:

- Round 1: K56 (63), bind off 18 stitches, knit to pen, eliminate the tag, knit to the beginning of neck bind off. 171 (192) stitches
- Note: From now on, you will function to and fro in rows, with each row ending at the neckline.
- Row 1 (wrong side): Bind off three stitches and purl to the end of the row. 168 (189) stitches
- Row 2 (best region): Bind off three stitches and knit to finish off-row. 165 (186) stitches
- Row 3: Bind off two stitches, purl to finish of row. 163 (184) stitches
- Row 4: Bind off two stitches and knit to finish off-row. 161 (182) stitches
- Row 5: P1, p2tog, purl to the last three stitches, p2tog via the back loophole (p2togtbl), p1. 159 (180) stitches
- Row 6: K1, SSK, knit to the last three stitches, k2tog, k1. 157 (178) stitches
- Row 7: P1, p2tog, repeat from to last four stitches, p1, p2togtbl, p1. 105 (119) stitches
- Row 8: Repeat Row 6. 103 (117) stitches
- Row 9: Purl.
- Repeat Rows 8 as well as likewise 9 two more times. 99 (113) stitches.
- Bind off freely.

Coating:

For the Bottom Edge:

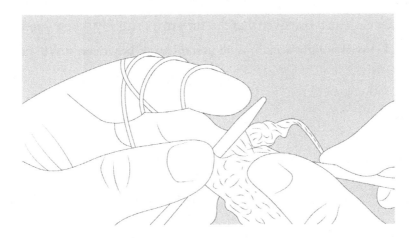

- Cast 3 stitches onto a dual sharp needle (for the neatest available finishing, utilize a Provisional Cast On).
- Weave an Attached I-cord around the lower hem of the sweater, getting one stitch for each cast-on stitch. (When you are completed: If you made use of a provisional cast, join the start and end of the I-cord with the Kitchener Stitch. If you cast on regularly, bind off the I-cord, stitch the beginning, and even finish with each other.).

For the Armhole Edges + Neckline:

- Similarly, knit Attached I-cords to the sleeve sides and around the neckline. Grab one stitch for every cast-on or abandoned stitch and, along the neckline, for each side stitch.

For the Weave + Block:

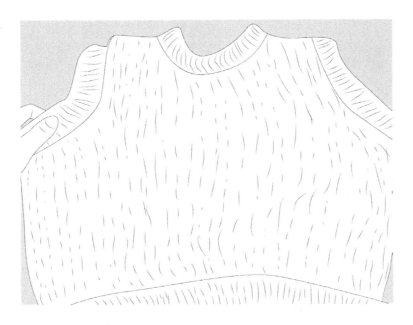

- Weave in the long run. Block your completed sweatshirt by first saturating it in area-temperature water and a light detergent (I love Soak since you don't have to rinse it!). Eject the excess water with your hands, then roll the coat in a dry towel. Finally, lay your sweatshirt flat on an additional, completely dry towel. You'll discover that the fur grows slightly when you block it and that the silk softens. Your jacket will not grow each time you clean it; however, it will continue to get softer and softer. Appreciate it!

4. Tie-Front Vest

Materials:

- Needles: US 10.5 or 6.5 mm
- Yarn: 5 bulky, four balls or skeins
- Extra: 2 stitch holders, yarn needle

Gauge and Size:

- Gauge: 14 S X 18 R in 4 inches using a stocking stitch
- Size: 28 inches

Instructions:

For Size Small:

1. Create the Back:

- Cast on 63 stitches.
- Row 1: On the right side, purl 1, knit 1, repeat four times, and then knit 6. Repeat this pattern four times, then purl 1, knit 1, and repeat three times, ending in 1 purl stitch.

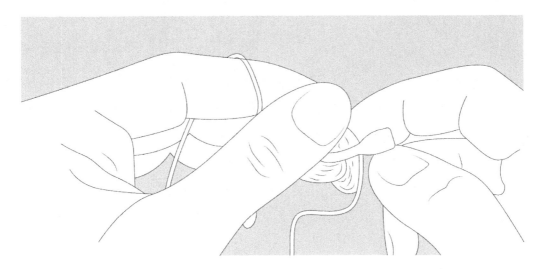

- Row 2: Knit 1, purl 1, repeat four times, and then purl 6. Repeat this pattern four times, then knit 1, purl 1, and repeat three times, ending in 1 knit stitch.
- Repeat Steps 2 and 3 until the project is 20 inches and ends with row 2.

2. Create the Shoulder Shape:

- Bind off eight stitches and begin the following four rows, keeping the 31 stitches on a stitch holder.

3. Create the Left Front:

- Cast on 32 stitches.
- Row 1: On the right side, knit 6. After that, knit 1, purl 1, and repeat four times. Repeat the whole set 2 times. End with knit one and purl 1 repeated two times.

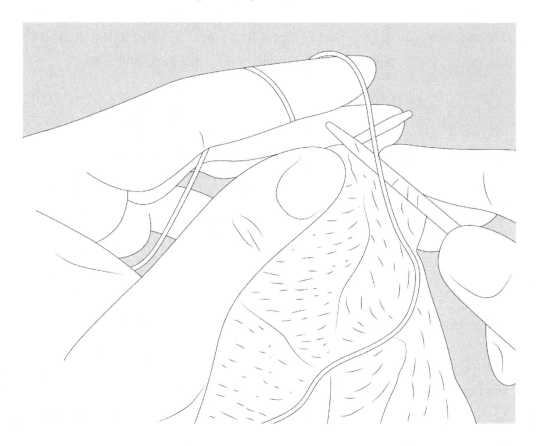

- Row 2: Knit 1 and purl 1 for two times. Knit 1, purl 1 four times, and then purl 6. Repeat the whole set of knit 1, purl 1 four times, and then purl 6 for two more times.
- Repeat Steps "b" and "c" until the project is 20 inches and ends with row 2.

4. Create the Shoulder Shape:

- Bind off eight stitches, begin the next, and follow with the alternate row, keeping the 16 stitches on a stitch holder.

5. Create the Right Front:

- Cast on 32 stitches.
- Row 1: On the right side, purl 1, knit 1, and repeat twice. Purl 1, knit 1 four times, and then knit 6. Repeat the whole purl one, knit 1 four times, and then knit 6 for two more times.
- Row 2: Purl 6. After, purl 1, knit 1, and repeat this four times. Repeat this whole set 2 times. Then purl 1, knit 1, and repeat two times.

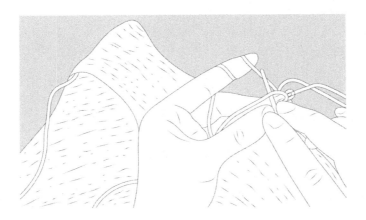

- Repeat Steps "b" and "c" until the project is 20 inches and ends with row 1.

6. Create the collar:

- Sew shoulder seams together.
- Place right sides together and work in purl 1. Knit one ribbing along the 16 stitches from the right front stitching holder, 31 stitches from the back stitching holder, and 16 stitches from the left front stitching holder. 63 total stitches.
- Continue ribbing for 7 inches. Bind off the ribbing.
- Insert markers on the edges of the back and front sides 8 inches below the shoulder seam.
- Sew the side seams from the casted edge to the markers using the yarn needle.

7. Create the ties:

- Cast on 60 stitches.
- Bind off.
- Repeat a second time.
- Attach the ties to the edges of the front in the middle, if desired.

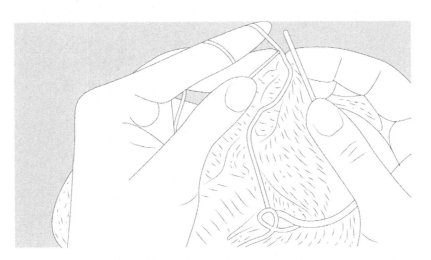

**Adjust for Larger Size:

For Size Medium:

Materials:

- Yarn: 5 balls or skeins

Instructions:

- Cast on (Back): 77 stitches.
- Row 1 (Back): Repeat five times.
- Row 2 (Back): Repeat five times.
- Shoulder Shape: Bind off ten stitches and leave 37 stitches for stitch holders.
- Cast on (Left Front): 36 stitches.
- Row 1 (L Front): Repeat twice and then four times.
- Row 2 (L Front): Repeat four times and then twice.
- Should Shape: Bind off ten stitches and leave 16 stitches for the stitch holder.
- Cast on (Right Front): 36 stitches.
- Row 1 (R Front): Repeat twice and then four times.
- Row 2 (R Front): Repeat four times and then two times.
- Collar, Step "b": Rib stitch 16 stitches, 37 stitches from the back stitching holder, and 16 stitches from the left front stitching holder. 69 total stitches.
- Collar, Step "d": 9 inches below.

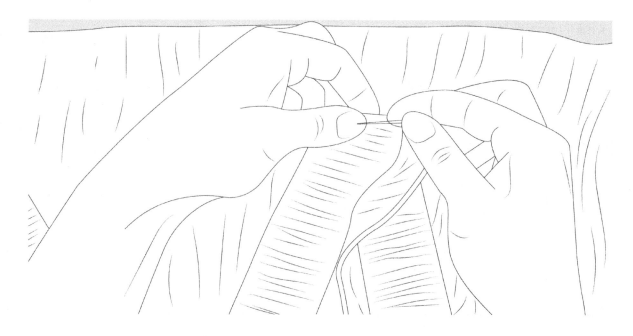

For Size Large:

Materials:

- Yarn: 6 balls or skeins.

Instructions:

- Cast on (Back): 91 stitches.
- Row 1 (Back): Repeat six times.
- Row 2 (Back): Repeat six times.
- Shoulder Shape: Bind off 13 stitches and leave 39 stitches for stitch holders.
- Cast on (Left Front): 44 stitches.
- Row 1 (L Front): Repeat 3 times and then one time.
- Row 2 (L Front): Repeat 1 time and then three times.
- Should Shape: Bind off 13 stitches and leave 18 stitches for the stitch holder.
- Cast on (Right Front): 44 stitches.
- Row 1 (R Front): Repeat twice and then once.
- Row 2 (R Front): Repeat 1 time and then three times.
- Collar, Step "b": Rib stitch 18 stitches, 39 stitches from the back stitching holder, and 18 stitches from the left front stitching holder. 75 total stitches.
- Collar, Step "d": 10 inches below.

For Size XL:

Materials:

- Yarn: 7 balls or skeins.

Instructions:

- Cast on (Back): 105 stitches.
- Row 1 (Back): Repeat seven times.
- Row 2 (Back): Repeat seven times.
- Shoulder Shape: Bind off 16 stitches and leave 41 stitches for stitch holders.
- Cast on (Left Front): 50 stitches.
- Row 1 (L Front): Repeat 3 times and then four times.
- Row 2 (L Front): Repeat 4 times and then three times.
- Should Shape: Bind off 16 stitches and leave 18 stitches for the stitch holder.
- Cast on (Right Front): 50 stitches.
- 1 (R Front): Repeat 3 times and then four times.
- Row 2 (R Front): Repeat once and then three times.
- Collar, Step "b": Rib stitch 18 stitches, 41 stitches from the back stitching holder, and 18 stitches from the left front stitching holder. 77 total stitches.
- Collar, Step "d": 10 inches below.

For Size 2XL:

Materials:

- Yarn: 8 balls or skeins.

Instructions:

- Cast on (Back): 119 stitches.
- Row 1 (Back): Repeat eight times.
- Row 2 (Back): Repeat eight times.
- Shoulder Shape: Bind off 19 stitches and leave 43 stitches for stitch holders.
- Cast on (Left Front): 58 stitches.
- Row 1 (L Front): Repeat 4 times and then one time.
- Row 2 (L Front): Repeat 1 time and then four times.
- Should Shape: Bind off 19 stitches and leave 20 stitches for the stitch holder.
- Cast on (Right Front): 58 stitches.

- Row 1 (R Front): Repeat four times and then one time.
- Row 2 (R Front): Repeat 1 time and then four times.
- Collar, Step "b": Rib stitch 20 stitches, 43 stitches from the back stitching holder, and 20 stitches from the left front stitching holder. 83 total stitches.
- Collar, Step "d": 10 inches below.

PART 4

KNITTING COLORFUL SHAWLS

CHAPTER 1:
GAUGE AND TECHNIQUES

Gauge

Check is only a proportion of how huge your lines are. The measure has two sections: join and lines. This implies check is estimating both the width of your fastens and the stature of your lines.

Not all knitters work in the same way; some of us tend to weave fastens more firmly, while others work exceptionally loosely. Since you cannot guarantee that your sewing system matches the creator's, taking measurements forces you to follow the architect's lead without making any changes to your sewing technique.

For what reason does a check make a difference?

You don't necessarily have to coordinate checks so far as you're set up for the outcomes.

You will need to coordinate a check to ensure that your fasten sizes match those of the creator if you are weaving a sweater with diverse sizes and need it to fit your 38-inch bust. In this manner, you understand that when you use the example, the bust will be 38 inches. If you don't, you can end up with a sweater that is either unusually huge or impossible to pull over your head. You may come up short on yarn or have extra yarn.

Let's say, for instance, that you buy a weaving bundle. The unit goes with the yarn; you may complete the task and create the largest size. However, if you are weaving fewer fasteners per inch than the amount shown in the sample, you'll run out of yarn before completing the project.

Then again, on the off chance that you are sewing a larger number of lines per inch than the check in the example, at that point, you will have far more yarn extra than you planned. This is particularly baffling when you can't return the yarn you've bought.

You can have the ideal amount of yarn if you take care to weave the proper amount. Otherwise, the project probably won't turn out the way that's been anticipated.

Measurement affects more than just fit and size. Looking closely at the Sand Stitch Hats, you'll see that the dark caps have been stitched together closely, creating a soft yet sturdy feel. However, the sea cap has a looser connection and a little more wrap. Sometimes a fashion designer deliberately wants free lines, but that is not the case with this cozy cap. The measurement not only affects how the cap fits on my head, but it also affects the shine. At the point when your lines are excessively free, cool air can sneak in, and you don't need that with this cap.

Step-By-Step Instructions To Get the Correct Gauge

So, you've chosen your need to get the correct check. Great decision! You have two choices:

- Simply start the task and measure as you go.

This choice can work for certain wearables like gloves and even caps. You can start the extend and measure the check or simply test the fit after a couple of rounds. Simply be set up to tear it out and begin once again if it doesn't fit.

- Weave a check swatch.

This is the most secure wager, particularly if you're taking a shot at a bigger venture like a sweater. Investigate your example and see what the check estimation is. The standard measure is four crawls by 4 inches; however, sometimes, it changes.

Cast on double the quantity of join that the measure calls for, utilizing the needles prescribed by the example. For instance, if the measure is 8, join for each inch, and cast on 16 lines. This will give you a huge swatch to gauge from.

Tip: I sewed the swatch presented above in the round since the cap design was in the round. I did this because my in-the-round sewing will generally be looser than my level of weaving. Repeat the line as intently as conceivable when swatching to get a precise number.

Weave until your swatch is around 6 inches tall to give you a large swatch to quantify. At that point, tie off.

The main thing you'll need to quantify is the number of lines. Lay your ruler or estimating tape over the focal point of the swatch and tally the number of lines that fit into 4 inches. This is your fasten measure.

Place the ruler vertically over your swatch and measure the number of columns that fit into 4 inches. This is your column check.

On the off chance you weave to check the first run-through, woohoo! You can go ahead and begin with your task.

Techniques

Increases and Decreases

While knitting and purling enable you to produce flat pieces, increases and decreases are required to shape hats, make a sweater, or craft a pair of socks. You will also use increases and decreases to work lace, from the simplest lace patterns to the most complex. Both increases and decreases can be worked flat or round in all knitting styles.

There are several different increases and decreases. Some leave an eyelet, or small hole in the knitting, while others lean in one direction. You can sometimes substitute one increase or decrease for another, but often knitting pattern designers have a reason for choosing one or the other.

The Yarn Over

The yarn over or "YO" is the simplest increase in knitting. Frequently used in lacework, the yarn over creates a rather large eyelet or hole. Make a yarn over by passing the yarn around the right-hand needle counterclockwise before knitting the next stitch on the needle. In most cases, you will knit this loose loop on the next row. Each yarn you make, as long as there is not a paired decrease, will add one stitch to the total stitch count on your needles.

The Knit Front and Back

The knit front and back or "KFB" increase produces a neat, even, and snug increase. While the M1L and M1R increases create a slight lean, the KFB leaves a small purl bump on the right side of your knitting.

When working a series of increases over multiple rows, these purl bumps can have a neat seam-like decorative effect.

Begin a KFB by knitting into the front loop of the stitch as usual. Do not slip the stitch from the left-hand needle. With the newly created stitch in place on the right-hand needle, point the tip of the right-hand needle down and knit into the back loop of the stitch.

Purl Front and Back

The purl front and back or PFB increase is similar to a KFB. Purl into the front loop, keeping the original stitch on the left-hand needle. Place the needle through the back loop, from back to front, and purl again. You now have two newly created stitches on the right-hand needle. Drop the worked stitch from the left-hand needle.

Long Tail Cast On

When fully acquainted with this method, it may be the only option you prefer for all your knitting projects. This long tail cast-on, or double cast-on method, is one of the fastest and most widely practiced methods among knitters. Whether you plan to knit the stretchy and tight border of socks or a hair band, it works wonderfully. Above all, it knits a neat and beautiful row which some knitters consider the first row of their project (though it is not). For this method, you need a little preparation. If you plan to create 15 stitches, add four to six inches of extra yarn with 15 inches of yarn and create a slip knot. Place the knot on the needle and hold the tail of the yarn with the left thumb and another part of the hanging yarn with the index finger of the left hand. Keep the fingers apart and hold the ends of the yarn with the other fingers. Now, place the knitting needle with the slip knot under the yarn between the thumb and finger and create a loop. Then, pull the thread of the yarn from the index finger through the loop, remove the thumb, and you will find a second stitch on the needle. Pull the yarn to fasten the knot and make sure not to make it too tight. The only disadvantage of this method is that if you fail to measure the yarn, you may run out in the middle of the work and have to start from the beginning.

CHAPTER 2:
PATTERNS AND PROJECTS

1. Fringed Triangle Shawl

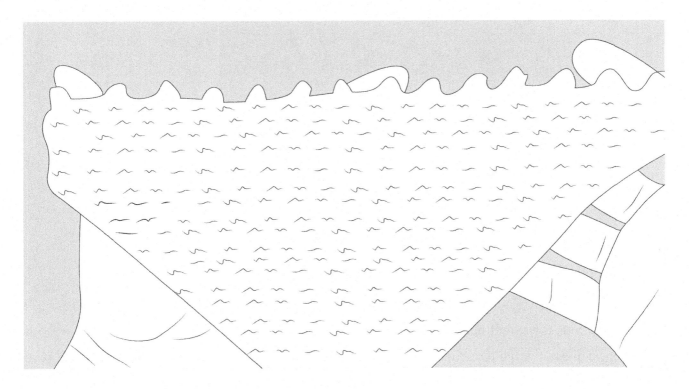

Materials:

- 2 hanks Plymouth Fantasy Naturale US 8 Circular needle (24")

Gauge:

- 4.5 stitches per inch on US 8 needles

Finished Size:

- 42" across the neck edge after blocking

Special Stitches:

- K1f&b: Knit into the front and the back of the next stitch to increase by 1.
- Ssk: slip one as if to knit, slip a second stitch as if to knit, return those two stitches to the left needle, and knit those two stitches through the back.

Instructions:

- Cast on eight stitches.
- Row 1: Knit.
- Set up pattern: Row 2: Right Side: K5, place marker, K1f&b, knit to end of row. Mark this side as the Right Side with a Locking stitch marker, coilless safety pin, or similar.

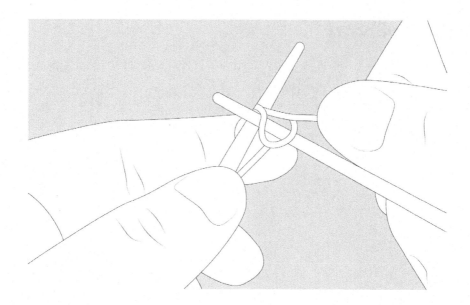

- Row 3: Knit all stitches.
- Begin pattern: Right Side rows (even-numbered): K5, slip marker, K1f&b, knit to end of row.
- Wrong Side rows (odd-numbered): Knit all stitches.
- Repeat these two pattern rows, increasing one stitch after the marker on the Right Side (even-numbered) rows by knitting into the front and the back of the next stitch.
- The first five stitches of every right-side row will always be knit even. This is the column of stitches you will later unravel or "drop" to create the fringe.
- Continue with pattern rows until the first skein has been used.
- Add a second skein and begin decreasing on all Right Side (even-numbered) rows as follows: Right Side rows (even-numbered): K5, slip marker, ssk, knit to the end.
- Wrong Side rows (odd-numbered): Knit all stitches.
- Continue decreasing until eight stitches remain. Knit one more wrong side row.
- On the next Right-Side row: K5, remove the marker. Bind off the remaining three stitches. Pull yarn through the last stitch and weave in the end.

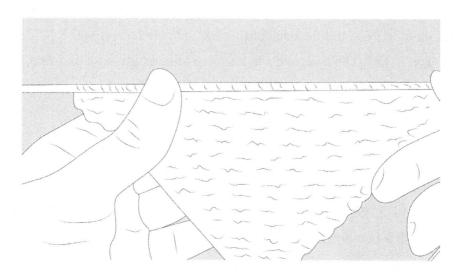

- Remove needles and drop all five stitches remaining.
- Gently unravel these stitches a few rows at a time, careful not to pull too hard. Make an overhand knot in each loop, pushing the knot up to the top of the loop nearest the shawl.

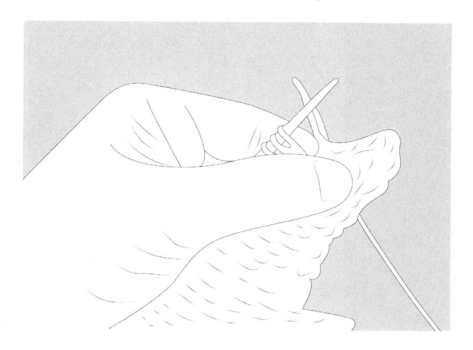

- Make sure the loops are all roughly the same length as the loops on either side before knotting each one.

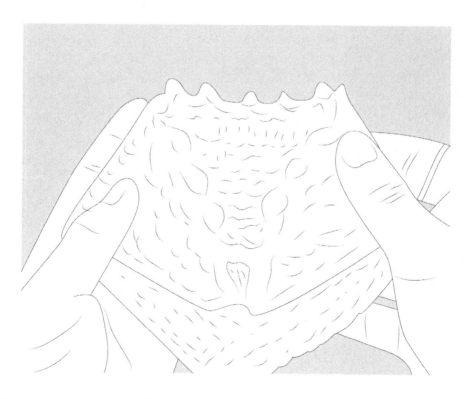

- Once all loops are unraveled and knotted, wet block the shawl and pin out to specified measurements. Dry thoroughly before removing the pins.

2. Scarf from Shawl-in-a-Ball!

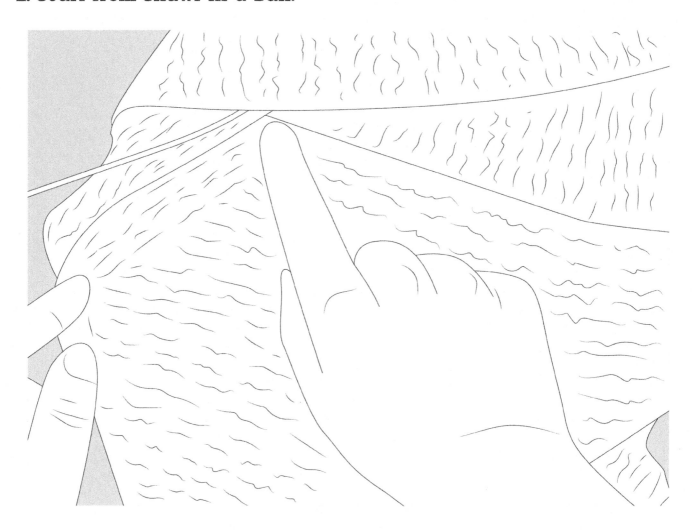

Materials:

- 5MM hook
- One skein of Shawl in a Ball (appr. 481 yards if using a different yarn)
- Scissors
- Tapestry needle

Instructions:

- Using the c2c method, we will start from the corner, going wider and wider until we are just about out of yarn.

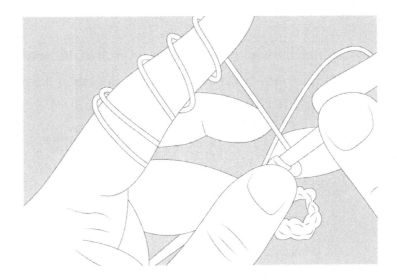

- Now for this pattern, we are not going to be decreasing. We are only increasing. Once you get the length, you will tie off (be sure to leave enough yarn to make tassels), and then you're done!

- CH 6

- DC into the 4th CH from the hook.

- DC in the next 2 CHs

- Turn. CH 6

- DC into the 4th CH from the hook. DC into the next 2 CHs.

- SL ST to TCH to join.

- CH 3

- 3 DC in TCH

- A Pattern for Shawl in the Ball Scarf:

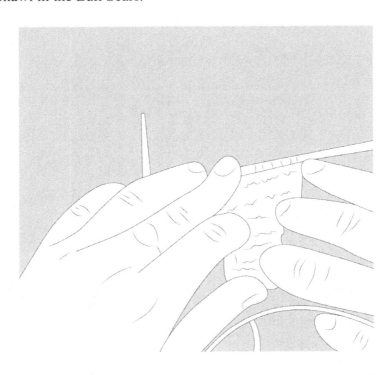

- CH 6
- R1 – DC into the 4th CH from the hook. Place one DC in each of the next two stitches. Turn.
- R2 – CH 6. In the 4th CH from the hook, place a DC. DC in each of the next two stitches (chains). Slip stitch to the TCH to join. CH 3. Place 3 DC in the THC. Turn.

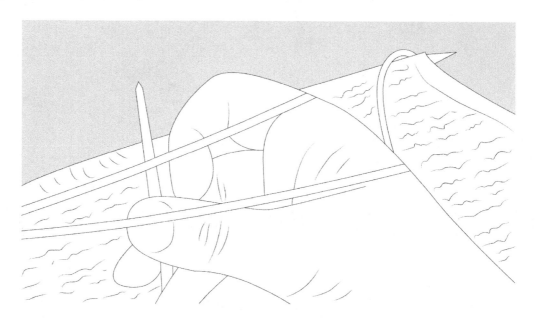

- R3 – CH 6. In the 4th CH from the hook, place a DC. DC in each of the next two stitches (chains). Slip stitch to the TCH to join. CH 3. Place 3 DC in the THC. Repeat from * to end. Turn.
- R4 – 43: repeat row 3. Tie off and weave in your ends.

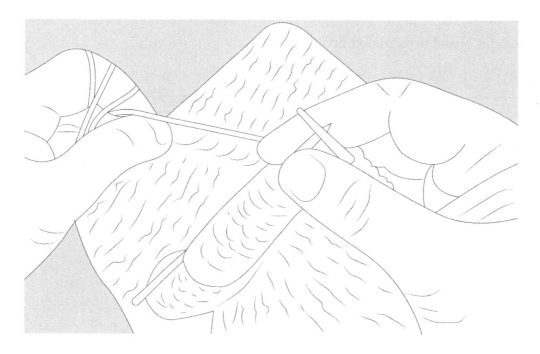

- Attach the tassels now at this point.

3. Flirty Shawl Knitting Pattern

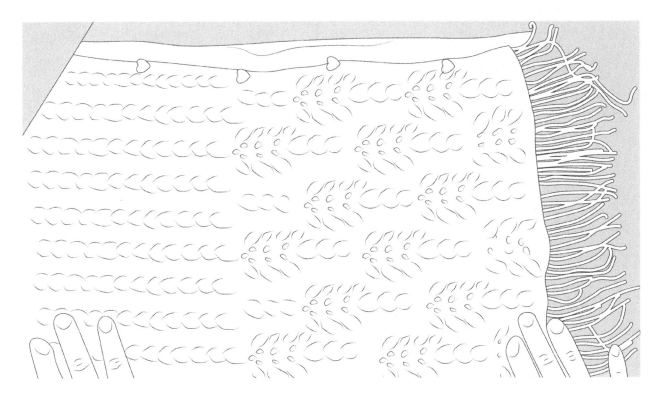

Materials:

- One ball of I Love This Yarn or Red Heart With Love – 4 medium – 6 ounces (approx. 170 yards)
- Q-hook 19/ 15.75mm
- Yarn Needle
- Scissors

Special Instruction:

- The pattern is worked back and forth without seams. Work in multiples of 2+4. The turning chain counts as a stitch. All double crochets are worked in the front loop only, except for the last double crochet of the row being worked in both loops of the 3rd ch of the turning ch.

Instructions for the Pattern:

- Row 1: Fsc 34, chain 4, turn

- Row 2-29: Skip 1, dc, chain 1, skip 1, dc, repeat from 15 times, chain 4, turn – 18sts

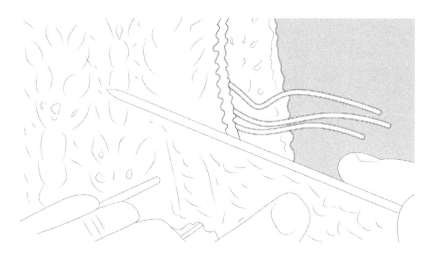

- Row 30: Skip 1, dc, chain 1, skip 1, dc, repeat from 15 times, chain 1, turn – 18sts

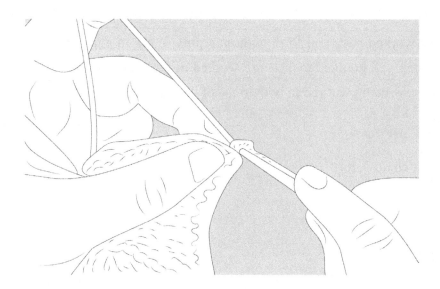

- Row 31: Sc across using both loops in each st across, fasten off, sew in the ends

4. Child's Poncho

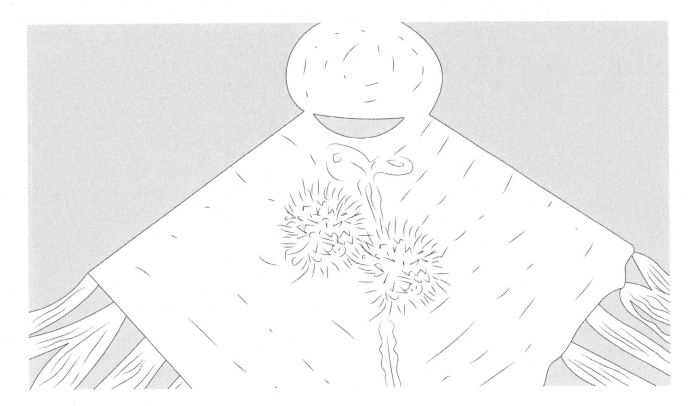

Material:

- Needles: US 8 or 5 mm
- Yarn: 5, bulky, up to 3 balls or skeins
- Extra: Yarn needle

Gauge and Size:

- Gauge: 15 S X 22 R in 4 inches with a stocking stitch
- Size: Up to 26.5 inches across chest X up to 17.5 inches long

Instructions (for 12 months size):

- Cast on 65 stitches.
- Row 1: On the wrong side, knit 1, purl 1, and knit 1. Repeat the purl one and knit one until the end of the row.

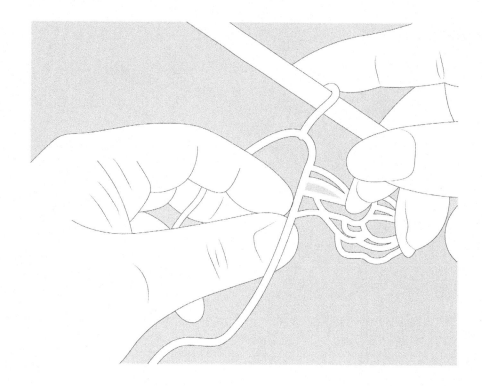

- Row 2: Knit one and two together on the right side, and repeat until the last four stitches. Slip 1, knit 1, pass the slipped stitch over, and finally knit 2.

- Row 3: Purl the entire row.

- Rows 4 to 6: Knit with a stocking stitch.

- Repeat Steps 4 and 5 ten times for 43 stitches.

- On the next row, on the right side, knit 2, knit two together, and knit until the last four stitches. Slip 1, knit 1, pass the slipped stitch over, and finally knit 2.

- Complete 1 row of purl stitches.

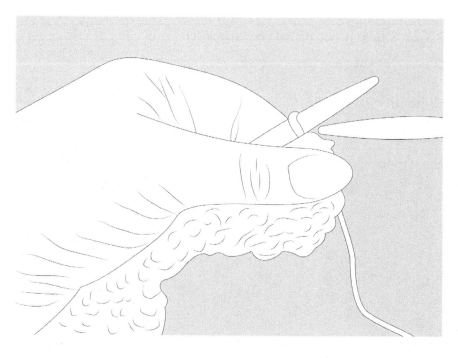

- Repeat the last two rows five times for 31 stitches.
- Bind off knitwise.
- Repeat for a second piece. Attach the center and back seams with the yarn needle, trim ends, and weave into the project.

**Adjust for Larger

Size 18 Months:

- Cast on 73 stitches.
- Step 6: Repeat 10 times for 51 stitches.
- Step 9: Repeat 9 times for 31 stitches.

Size 2/4:

- Cast on 85 stitches.
- Step 6: Repeat 10 times for 63 stitches.
- Step 9: Repeat 14 times for 33 stitches.

Size 6/8:

- Cast on 97 stitches.
- Step 6: Repeat 10 times for 75 stitches.

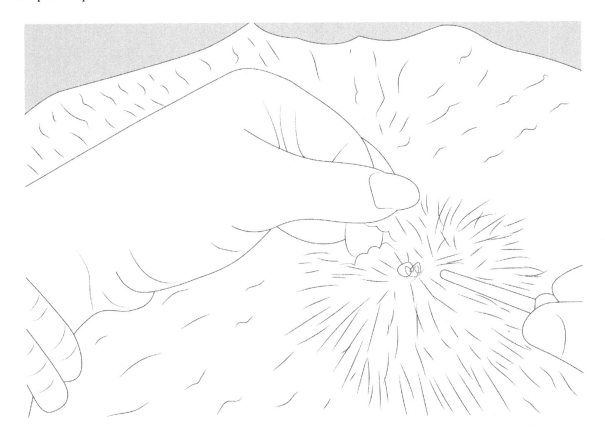

- Step 9: Repeat 19 times for 35 stitches.

5. Easy Knit Shawl

Material:

- 480 yards of yarn
- Stitch marker
- Tapestry needle
- US Size 8 circular 40" needle

Gauge:

- 4 stitches per inch

Size:

- Adult

Instructions:

- Make a loop for a slip knot. Run it through the sewing needle with the tail in front. Make it tight. You are going to cast three stitches on it now. There is already one stitch on the needle in this situation. Consider that slip knot as the first stitch.

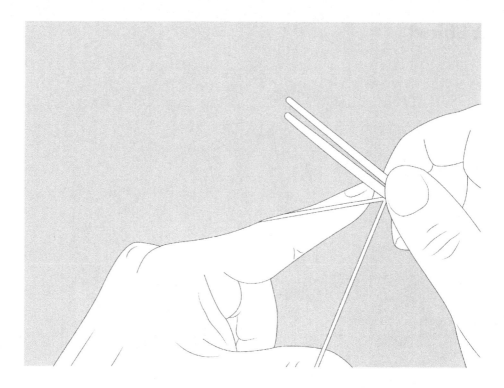

2. To cast the two following stitches, use the long tail technique.

- Take the need, go in between the tail and the yarn ball, and then make the rest of the stitches.
- Have your thumb rest on the tail and a finger on the yarn ball's yarn. Holding this thread, holding the stitch to stabilize it. Turn your finger and thumb back. Go in under your thumb, then go over your finger.

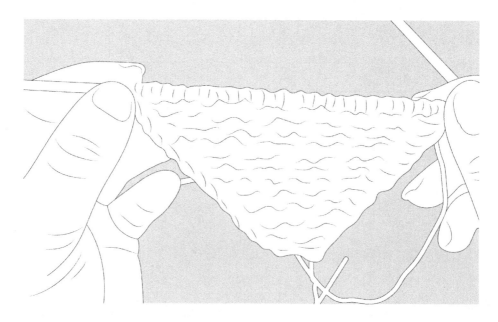

- Finish by going back through the hole where your thumb was, and your second stitch is done. Lean them over your finger under your palm, back into your thumb, and tighten. And your three stitches are there.

3. Treat the circular needle like a straight one and knit your first row that way.

- The pattern increases at the start of this row, and you just knit straight through the next row. In this first stitch, begin the increase.

- Put the right needle behind the left, knit the stitch, and slip it off the needle instead of sliding it off.

- You should see a purl bump now that an increase has been made. Then you just need to knit the remaining stitches in a row. Continue knitting row after row, adding an increase at the beginning of each one.

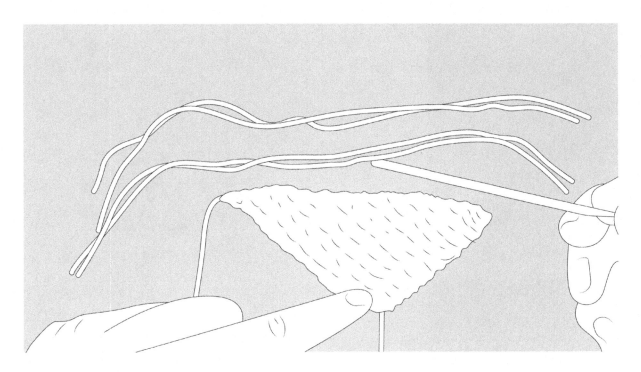

4. Once the shawl reaches your desired size, it is time to start binding.

5. Knit the first stitch, followed by a second stitch.

- Take the first stitch over the second stitch. Then repeat across the final row. Be mindful not to knit this step too tightly, as the average length of that side of the shawl will be tight, and it will look awkward. Some people turn to another needle if they have trouble casting out too tight. It could be one or two sizes bigger, so they do not have this problem. So, if you feel tight, try this and see if you can manage better.

6. If you do not want to use the above option, try to give a little extra slack, and do not pull up for every stitch.

7. Pull the yarn end and run it through the final loop to knit the last stitch.

8. You are going to weave in the ends of the thread. Here is where you will use the tapestry needle to finish the shawl.

9. Weave the needle in a garter pattern. Follow the purl bumps lines.

- Depending on how much thread you have left, you do it for maybe 4 to 6 stitches. The intention is to make it so entrenched that this thread will not come loose and unravel. Go back through a couple of stitches if you need to.

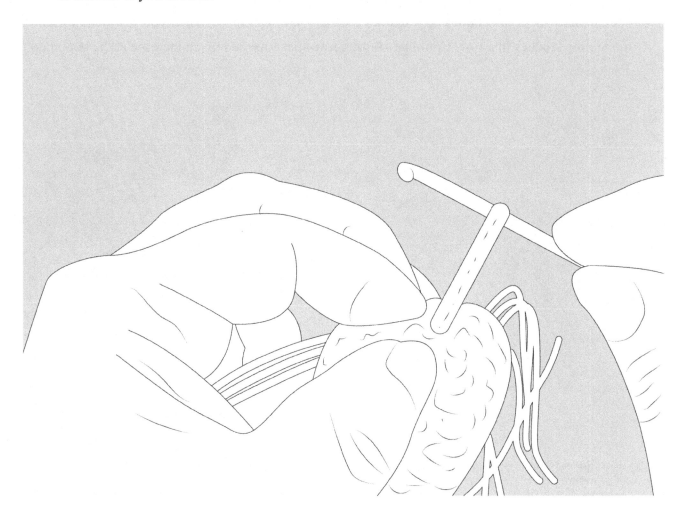

- Then, go back in the opposite direction, a few stitches, and follow, and that is it. Cut the thread very close to the end of the job, being careful not to cut the work.

And there you go, a nice shawl to wear out that you made yourself. Great!

6. Autumn Shawl

Materials:

- Two balls of Bernat® Satin Yarn (100 g/3.5 oz; 149 m/163 yds) in the following colors:
  - E: Rouge
  - D: Cameo
  - C: Amber
  - B: Buff
  - A: Mocha

Size:

- 5.5 mm (U.S. I or 9) crochet hook or size needed to obtain gauge

Measurements:

- Approx 24 x 70 ins [61 x 178 cm].

Gauge:

- 13 sc and 14 rows = 4 ins [10 cm]

Instructions:

Stripe Pat: Work 2 rows of each color in the following sequence: A, B, C, A, D, E. These 12 rows form Stripe Pat.

The shawl is worked widthwise.

- With A, ch 227.

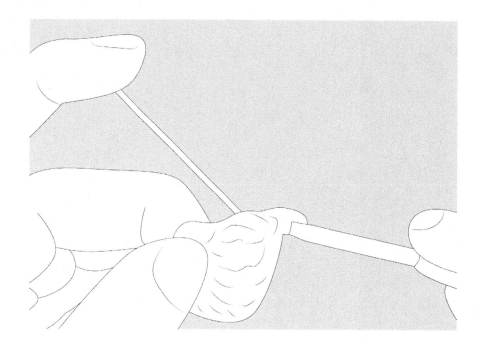

- 1st row: (RS). One sc in 2nd ch from hook. 1 sc in each ch to end of ch. 226 sc. Turn.

- 2nd and alt rows: Ch 2 (does not count as st). 1 hdc in each st to end of row. Join B. Turn.

- First two rows of Stripe Pat are completed.

- 3rd row: With B, ch 1. 1 sc in each of the first three hdc. (Pulling long loop, one sc in next foundation ch two rows below – long sc made) twice. 1 sc in each of the next two hdc. Rep from to last three hdc. 1 sc in each of the last three hdc. Turn.

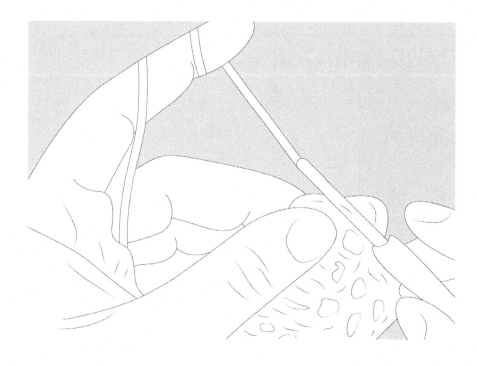

- 5th row: With C, Ch 1. 1 sc in the first hdc. Long sc in each of the next two hdc two rows below. 1 sc in each of the next two hdc. Rep from ending with one sc in the last hdc. Join A. Turn.

- 7th row: With A, ch 1. 1 sc in each of the first three hdc. Long sc in each of the next two hdc two rows below. 1 sc in each of the next two hdc. Rep from to last three hdc. 1 sc in each of the last three hdc. Turn.

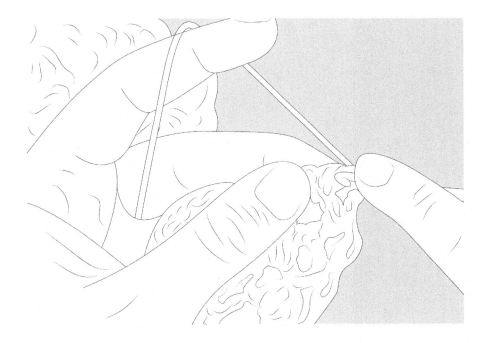

- 8th row: As 2nd row joining D at the end of row.

- Keeping cont of Stripe Pat, rep 5th to 8th rows for pat until work from beg measures approx 24 ins [61 cm], ending with a WS row. Fasten off.

- Finishing: With RS facing, join A with sl st to the left corner of the side edge. Work in sc across the side edge of the Shawl. Fasten off. Rep across another side.

7. Waning Moon Shawl

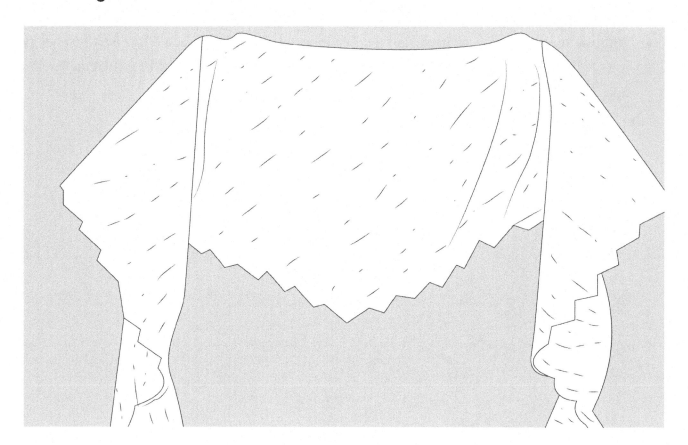

Materials:

- Needles: US 5 or 3.75 mm
- Yarn: Fingerling weight, 200 yards
- Extra: Blocking pins

Gauge and Size:

- Gauge: 19 S X 36 R in 4 inches, textured pattern after blocking
- Size: 70-inch long x 13 inches at the longest point

Instructions:

1. Longtail cast on 12 stitches.

2. Knit 2 rows.

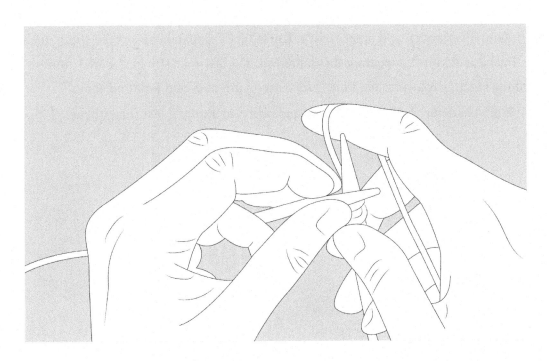

3. Knit the waning moon pattern:

- Row 1: On the right side, knit 1, yarn over, and repeat twice. Knit to the front and back of the stitch, then knit to the last three stitches. Knit to the stitch's front and back, yarn over, and knit 1, repeating yarn over and knit one again.
- Row 2: On the wrong side, knit 3, purl to the last three stitches, and knit 3.

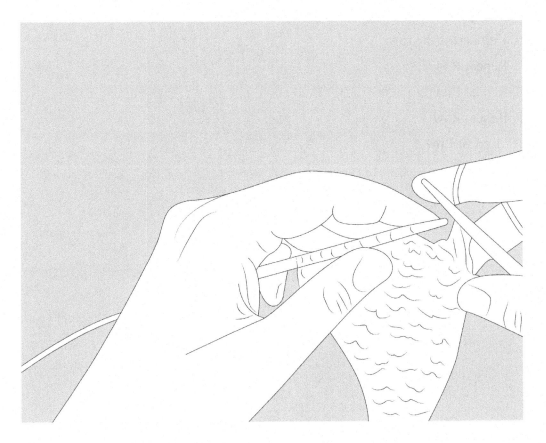

- Row 3: Knit 1, yarn over, and repeat twice. Knit to the front and back of the stitch, then purl one and knit 1. Purl 2 and knit 2, repeating this pattern to the last four stitches. Purl 1, knit to the front and back of the stitch, yarn over, and knit 1, repeating yarn over and knit one again.
- Row 4: Knit 4 and purl 1. Repeat knit two and purl one until the last four stitches. Finish with knit 4.

- Row 5: Knit 1, yarn over, and repeat twice. Knit to the front and back of the stitch, purl 1, yarn over, slip, slip, knit, knit two together, and yarn over. Purl 2, yarn over, slip, slip, knit, knit two together, and yarn over, repeating this pattern to the last four stitches. Purl 1, knit to the front and back of the stitch, repeat yarn over, and knit 1 two times.
- Row 6: Knit across the row.
- Row 7: Repeat Row 1.
- Row 8: Repeat Row 2.
- Row 9: Repeat Row 3.
- Row 10: Repeat Row 4.

- Row 11: Knit 1, yarn over, and repeat twice. Knit to the front and back of the stitch. Knit 2 together, yarn over, purl 2, yarn over, slip, slip, and knit, repeating this pattern to the last three stitches. Knit to the front and back of the stitch. Finish with yarn over and knit 1, repeating two times.
- Row 12: Knit across the row.

4. Repeat Step 3 at least nine times or until the shawl is your desired length.

5. Create the border:

- Repeat Rows 1 and 2 of the Waning Moon pattern.
- Row 3: Knit 3, purl to the front and back of the stitch, and knit 1. Purl to the front and back of the stitch two times and then knit 1. Repeat purl to the front and back of the stitch two times and then knit one until the last four stitches. Finish by purling to the front and back of the stitch and then knit 3.
- Row 4: Knit 5 and purl 1. Knit 4, purl 1, and repeat this pattern until the last five stitches. Finish with knit 5.
- Row 5: Knit 2, purl 2, and knit 1. Purl 4, knit 1, and repeat this pattern until the last five stitches. Finish with purl two and knit 3.
- Row 6: Repeat Row 4.
- Row 7: Knit across the row.
- Row 8: Knit 3, purl to the last three stitches, and knit 3.
- Row 9: Knit across the row.

- Row 10: On the wrong side, bind off knitwise.

PART 5

KNITTING ANIMAL PATTERNS

CHAPTER 1:
GAUGE AND TECHNIQUES

Gauge

Knitting gauges is a handy tool, especially as you move on to more complex patterns. It's the number of stitches it'll take to make up four inches (10cms) of fabric. It'll often be given in two different measurements, showing how many stitches will be across the four inches and how many rows of fabric will be there.

You can buy a special knitting gauge ruler, but you can also use just a four-inch ruler. You'll want to place the fabric onto a flat surface and then flatten it out to measure it. It should not be curled. To measure, the ruler must be placed flat across the fabric with the first tick lined up with your very first stitch. Count up to one inch, then multiply by four, and you'll get the gauge of your fabric.

Techniques

Cast On

Before you attempt any animal knitting, you must first cast on. Casting on means getting your yarn and needles ready to start knitting. You are creating loops along your needle that will become the initial row of stitching. There are a few methods people use to cast on:

- Single
- Longtail
- Knitted
- Cable

Single and Longtail are great beginner cast-on techniques, but you should practice each method to find what you like the best. Regardless of your chosen method, you need to start with a slip-knot. To create these slipknots, follow these simple instructions:

- Make a loop with your yarn and bring the tail through the loop to create a second loop. This will create a knot at the end.
- Slide it onto your needle and pull it to tighten. That is it!

Now, try out the different cast-on methods by following the instructions below:

Knit Stitch

Next up is the knit stitch. This is also important because it is the base for knitting projects such as making scarves or washcloths. If you know how to do the cast on, you will have no problems doing this.

- You have to "open loops" in this step. To do this, you must make sure that you use both the needles in your left and right hands and focus on the back of the yarn. The stitches you'll be making should now be facing you, with the lumps facing the front of your body. Work on single loops only.
- You should then slip the needle on your right hand into the first loop. After that, just loop the working yarn over the right-hand needle in a counter-clockwise direction so that it slips between your two fingers. This will help you out a lot in completing your desired projects.
- Next, slide the right-hand needle from front to back and keep the loop of the yarn on the right-hand side. One easy way to do this is by letting the yarn slip through the top of the right-hand needle and just pushing it a bit.
- To finish this stitch, you'd have to slide the right-hand needle up so that the first loop from the left-hand side would slip right through it. This way, you can be sure that the loop has worked. Do the same thing with the loop, on the other hand, too. You can flip the work over so that the same results would be seen on the other side of the yarn. Move the yarn from right to left to see what will happen.

Purling

The third basic step that you would have to learn is Purling. This is what is known as the opposite of the Knit Stitch.

- To do this, you should open the first loop on the needle, which is situated in your left hand, and ensure that the empty needle is on the right. But, instead of working on the back of the yarn to create lumps, you should now focus on working on the front side of the yarn.
- Move the working yarn over the first loop of the needle in your left hand and then take the working yarn over the second needle to create a Knit stitch. Work on this in counter-clockwise motion but see that the lumps appear in front, not at the back.
- Make sure the yarn has gone between two needles, and then make the new loop using the right-hand needle. Now, switch the needles' places to move the left-hand loop to the right-hand one.
- Slide the right-hand needle back into the loop and then let it slide past the left-hand needle so that the new loop would be on the right-hand needle, and the working yarn will now be in front.
- The combination of knitting and purling would allow you to create beautiful projects. See? It's not that hard.

Binding It Off

The final part of the basic knitting method is called "Binding Off" or "Casting Off". This means that you know will have to learn how to close the loops so that you can get them off the needles and so that you can finally say that the project is now complete.

- Once you have knitted and purled the last row of the piece of cloth you are making, start purling or knitting the last two stitches of that row and make sure they are now on the right-hand side.
- Then, use the tip of the left-hand needle to pull up the first stitch over the second stitch of the right-hand needle. This will then leave you with one stitch. Repeat the process until you are left with no more stitches on the left-hand side and just one stitch on the right.
- Now, slip this last piece of stitch through the needle. It would be good to trim your working yarn so that you only have a few inches left to loop into your finished work. Slip the said yarn over the loop and pull tightly. This way, you can be sure that the yarn will not unravel.
- Next, weave the yarn in several stitches over the loop using a crochet hook or a sewing needle. That's it. You are now able to close the loop and will now be able to finish your project.

Joining Yarns and Working with Color

Joining a new ball of yarn is a must when the old one runs out. It's best to join the new yarn at the beginning of a row. Pick up the new yarn and continue knitting if the yarn needs to be joined in the middle of the row. Darn in the ends of the new and old yarns neatly behind the work after you have knitted a few more rows.

Long Tail Cast-On

To ensure you have a long enough tail to cast on your stitches, wrap the yarn around the needle the same amount of times as the number of stitches you need, plus about 25cm (10in) extra to use for sewing up later if needed.

- Make a slip knot (A).
- With the needle in your right hand, keeping the ball end closest to you, place your left thumb and forefinger between the two strands of yarn. Grasp the loose ends with your other fingers and hold them in your palm (B).
- Spread your thumb and forefinger apart to make the yarn taut, then move your thumb up towards the tip of the needle, keeping your palm facing forwards (C).
- Bring the needle tip up through the loop on your thumb (D).
- Then, over the top and around the yarn on your forefinger (E).
- Take the needle back through the thumb loop (insert from the top) (F).
- Gently pull your thumb out and pull on the tail ends to tighten the stitch (G).
- Repeat steps 3-7 (H).

Stripes

When working stripes, carry the yarn up the side of the work. Simply drop the old color at the back of the work and pick the new color to work the first stitch (A). For thicker stripes (more than four rows), catch the old yarn every couple of rows by twisting it with the working yarn (B).

CHAPTER 2:
PATTERNS AND PROJECTS

1. Squirrel

Materials:

For the Body:

- Scheepjes Stonewashed (50g/130m; 78% cotton/22% acrylic) yarn in the following shades:
  - Yarn A Orange (Coral 816), two balls
  - Yarn B Cream (Moonstone 801), one ball
- 2.75mm (US 2) straight needles
- Toy stuffing
- 2 x 10mm (1â□„2in) buttons
- Scrap piece of 4-ply yarn for embroidering the nose

For the Outfit:

- Scheepjes Catona (10g/25m, 25g/62m, or 50g/125m; 100% cotton) yarn in the following shades:
  - Yarn A Cream (Old Lace 130), 1 x 50g ball
  - Yarn B Dark Blue (Light Navy 164), 1 x 50g ball
  - Yarn C Green (Sage Green 212), 1 x 50g ball

- 2.75mm (US 2) straight needles
- 3mm (US 2) straight needles
- 3mm (US 2) circular needle (23cm/9in length)
- Set of four 3mm (US 2) double-pointed needles
- 3.5mm (US 4) straight needles
- 3.5mm (US 4) circular needle (23cm/9in length)
- Set of four 3.5mm (US 4) double-pointed needles
- Cable needle
- Waste yarn
- 11 small buttons

Before you start, read the Essential Notes at the beginning of this book.

Instructions for the Squirrel Body:

For the Head:

Starting at the neck:

- Using Yarn A and 2.75mm straight needles, cast on 11 sts.
- Row 1 (ws): Purl.

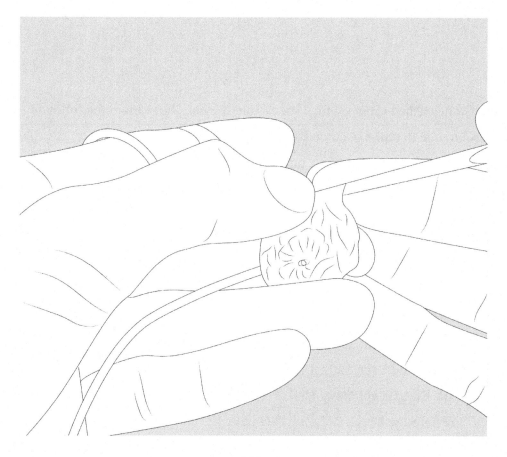

- Row 2: [K1, M1] to last st, K1. (21 sts)

- Row 3: Purl.

- Row 4: [K2, M1] to last st, K1. (31 sts)

- Row 5: Purl.

- Row 6: K1, m1l, knit to last st, m1r, K1. (33 sts) Row 7: Purl.

- Row 8: [K1, m1l, K15, m1r] twice, K1. (37 sts) Row 9: Purl.

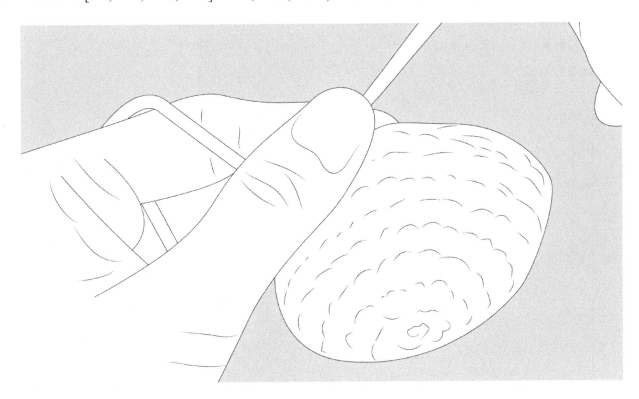

- Row 10: [K1, m1l, K17, m1r] twice, K1. (41 sts) Row 11: P20, m1pl, P1, m1pr, P20. (43 sts) Row 12: (A) K1, m1l, K20, m1r, (B) K1, (A) m1l, K20, m1r, K1. (47 sts) Row 13: (A) P23, (B) m1pl, P1, m1pr, (A) P23. (49 sts) Row 14: (A) K22, (B) K2, m1r, K1, m1l, K2, (A) K22. (51 sts) Row 15: (A) P21, (B) P9, (A) P21.

- Row 16: (A) K1, m1l, K20, (B) K4, m1r, K1, m1l, K4, (A) K20, m1r, K1. (55 sts) Row 17: (A) P22, (B) P11, (A) P22.

- Row 18: (A) K22, (B) K5, sl1, K5, (A) K22.

- Row 19: (A) P22, (B) P11, (A) P22.

- Row 20: (A) K23, (B) K4, sl1, K4, (A) K23.

- Continue in Yarn A only.

- Row 21: Purl.

- Row 22: K26, CDD, K26. (53 sts)

- Row 23: Purl.

- Row 24: K25, CDD, K25. (51 sts)

- Row 25: Purl.
- Row 26: K24, CDD, K24. (49 sts)
- Row 27: Purl.
- Row 28: K1, K2tog, K20, CDD, K20, SSK, K1. (45 sts) Row 29: Purl.
- Row 30: K21, CDD, K21. (43 sts)
- Row 31: Purl.
- Row 32: K1, K2tog, K17, CDD, K17, SSK, K1. (39 sts) Row 33: Purl.
- Row 34: K19, sl1, K19.
- Row 35: Purl.

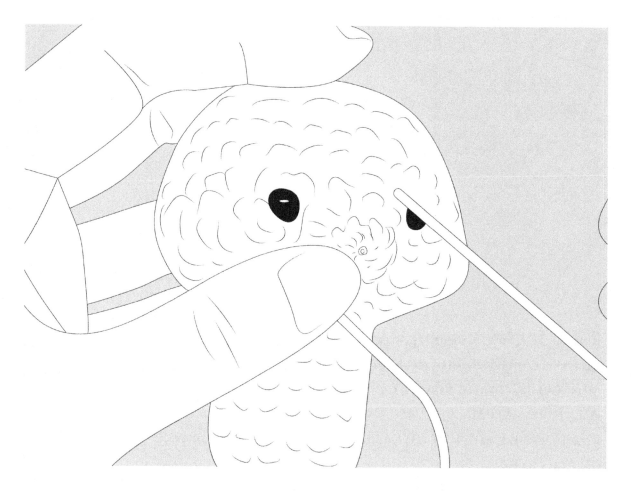

- Row 36: K1, K2tog, K16, sl1, K16, SSK, K1. (37 sts) Row 37: Purl.
- Row 38: K18, sl1, K18.
- Row 39: Purl.
- Row 40: K1, K2tog, K3, K2tog 4 times, K3, CDD, K3, SSK 4 times, K3, SSK, K1. (25 sts) Row 41: Purl.
- Row 42: K1, K2tog 5 times, CDD, SSK 5 times, K1. (13 sts) Row 43: Purl.
- Cast off.

For the Ears (Make 2):

- Using Yarn A and 2.75mm straight needles, cast on 14 sts.
- Row 1 (ws): Purl.
- Row 2: K5, [K1, M1] 3 times, knit to end. (17 sts)
- Rows 3-7: Stocking stitch five rows.

- Row 8: [K3, K2tog, SSK] twice, K3. (13 sts) Row 9: Purl.
- Row 10: K1, [K1, K2tog, SSK] twice, K2. (9 sts) Row 11: Purl.
- Row 12: K1, K2tog, sl1 kw, K2tog, PSSO, SSK, K1. (5 sts) Row 13: Purl.
- Row 14: Knit.
- Cut yarn, leaving a long tail. Using a tapestry needle, thread the tail through the stitches left on the needle and pull up tight to gather stitches.

For the Tail:

- Using Yarn A and 2.75mm straight needles, cast on 25 sts.
- Row 1 (ws): P3, turn.
- Row 2: YO, K3.
- Row 3: P3, SSP, P1, turn.
- Row 4: YO, K5.
- Row 5: P5, SSP, P1, turn.

- Row 6: YO, K7.
- Row 7: P7, SSP, P1, turn.
- Row 8: YO, K9.
- Row 9: P9, SSP, P1, turn.
- Row 10: YO, K11.
- Row 11: P11, SSP, purl to end.
- Row 12: K3, turn.
- Row 13: YO, P3.
- Row 14: K3, K2tog, K1, turn.
- Row 15: YO, P5.
- Row 16: K5, K2tog, K1, turn.
- Row 17: YO, P7.
- Row 18: K7, K2tog, K1, turn.
- Row 19: YO, P9.
- Row 20: K9, K2tog, K1, turn.
- Row 21: YO, P11.
- Row 22: K11, K2tog, knit to end.
- Rows 23-66: Rpt Rows 1-22 twice more.
- Rows 67-75: Stocking stitch nine rows.

- Row 76: [K1, m1l, K11, m1r] twice, K1. (29 sts)

- Rows 77-87: Stocking stitch 11 rows.

- Row 88: [K1, m1l, K13, m1r] twice, K1. (33 sts)

- Rows 89-99: Stocking stitch 11 rows.

- Row 100: [K1, m1l, K15, m1r] twice, K1. (37 sts) Row 101: Purl.

- Row 102: K35, turn.

- Row 103: YO, P33, turn.

- Row 104: YO, K31, turn.

- Row 105: YO, P29, turn.

- Row 106: YO, K27, turn.

- Row 107: YO, P25, turn.

- Row 108: YO, K23, turn.

- Row 109: YO, P21, turn.

- Row 110: YO, P19, turn.

- Row 111: YO, P17, turn.

- Row 112: YO, K15, turn.

- Row 113: YO, P13, turn.

- Row 114: YO, K13, [K2tog, K1] to end.

- Row 115: P25, [SSP, P1] to end.

- Rows 116-143: Rpt Rows 102-115 twice more.

- Rows 144-145: Stocking stitch two rows.

- Row 146: K1, K2tog, K31, SSK, K1. (35 sts) Row 147: Purl.

- Row 148: K16, CDD, K16. (33 sts)

- Row 149: Purl.

- Row 150: K1, K2tog, K27, SSK, K1. (31 sts) Row 151: Purl.

- Row 152: K14, CDD, K14. (29 sts)

- Row 153: Purl.

- Row 154: K1, K2tog, K10, CDD, K10, SSK, K1. (25 sts) Row 155: Purl.

- Row 156: K11, CDD, K11. (23 sts)

- Row 157: Purl.

- Row 158: K10, CDD, K10. (21 sts)

- Row 159: Purl.

- Row 160: K9, CDD, K9. (19 sts)

- Row 161: P8, PCDD, P8. (17 sts)

- Row 162: K7, CDD, K7. (15 sts)
- Row 163: P6, PCDD, P6. (13 sts)
- Row 164: K5, CDD, K5. (11 sts)
- Row 165: P4, PCDD, P4. (9 sts)
- Row 166: K3, CDD, K3. (7 sts)
- Row 167: P2, PCDD, P2. (5 sts)
- Rows 168-169: Stocking stitch two rows.
- Cut yarn, leaving a long tail. Using a tapestry needle, thread the tail through the stitches left on the needle and pull up tight to gather stitches.

For the Body:

- Work as Standard Body - Contrast Front.

For the Arms (Make 2):

- Work as Standard Arms

For the Legs (Make 2):

- Work as Standard Legs - Plain
- Making Up
- Follow the instructions in the techniques section (see Techniques: Making Up Your Animal).

Instructions for the Outfit:

For the Tie T-Shirt:

The T-shirt is worked top down, with raglan sleeves. It is worked back and forth in rows with a button band opening and seam at the back; the sleeves are worked in the round. The tie motif is worked using the Intarsia method (see Techniques: Colorwork).

- Using 3mm straight needles and Yarn A, cast on 31 sts.
- Row 1 (ws): Knit.
- Row 2 (buttonhole row): K1, YO, K2tog, knit to end.
- Row 3: Knit.
- Row 4: K3, [K1, K1fb, K1] to last four sts, K4. (39 sts) Change to 3.5mm straight needles.

The Tie Chart is worked over the next 31 rows in stocking stitch and using the Intarsia method (see Techniques: Colorwork). Starting at the bottom left of the chart, read WS rows from left to right and RS rows from right to left.

- Row 5: K3, P5, pm, P6, pm, P2, work Tie Chart, P3, pm, P6, pm, P4, K3.
- Row 6: [Knit to marker, m1r, sm, K1, m1l] twice, K2, work Tie Chart, [knit to marker, m1r, sm, K1, m1l] knit to end. (47 sts) Row 7: K3, P17, work Tie Chart, purl to last 3 sts, K3.
- Row 8: [Knit to marker, m1r, sm, K1, m1l] twice, K3, work Tie Chart, [knit to marker, m1r, sm, K1, m1l] knit to end. (55 sts) Row 9: K3, P21, work Tie Chart, purl to last 3 sts, K3.
- Row 10 (buttonhole row): K1, YO, K2tog, [knit to marker, m1r, sm, K1, m1l] twice, K4, work Tie Chart, [knit to marker, m1r, sm, K1, m1l] twice, knit to end. (63 sts) Row 11: K3, P25, work Tie Chart, purl to last 3 sts, K3.
- Row 12: [Knit to marker, m1r, sm, K1, m1l] twice, K5, work Tie Chart, [knit to marker, m1r, sm, K1, m1l] knit to end. (71 sts) Row 13: K3, P29, work Tie Chart, purl to last 3 sts, K3.
- Row 14: [Knit to marker, m1r, sm, K1, m1l] twice, K6, work Tie Chart, [knit to marker, m1r, sm, K1, m1l] knit to end. (79 sts) Row 15: K3, P33, work Tie Chart, purl to last 3 sts, K3.
- Row 16: [Knit to marker, m1r, sm, K1, m1l] twice, K7, work Tie Chart, [knit to marker, m1r, sm, K1, m1l] knit to end. (87 sts) Row 17: K3, P37, work Tie Chart, purl to last 3 sts, K3.
- Row 18 (buttonhole row): K1, YO, K2tog, [knit to marker, m1r, sm, K1, m1l] twice, K8, work Tie Chart, [knit to marker, m1r, sm, K1, m1l] twice, knit to end. (95 sts) Row 19: K3, P41, work Tie Chart, purl to last 3 sts, K3.
- Row 20: [Knit to marker, m1r, sm, K1, m1l] twice, K9, work Tie Chart, [knit to marker, m1r, sm, K1, m1l] knit to end. (103 sts) Row 21: K3, P45, work Tie Chart, purl to last 3 sts, K3.
- Row 22: [Knit to marker, m1r, sm, K1, m1l] twice, K10, work Tie Chart, [knit to marker, m1r, sm, K1, m1l] knit to end. (111 sts) Row 23: Cast off three sts, P49 (this includes the st from the last cast off), work Tie Chart, purl to last three sts, K3. (108 sts) Row 24: Knit to marker, remove marker, K1, m1a (right back). Without working them, place the next 23 sts onto waste yarn (sleeve), sm, m1a, K12, work Tie Chart, knit to marker, remove marker, K1, m1a (front), without working them place next 23 sts onto waste yarn (sleeve), sm, m1a, knit to end (left back). (66 sts) Row 25: P28, work Tie Chart, purl to end.
- Row 26: Knit to 1 st before marker, m1r, K1, sm, K1, m1l, K12, work Tie Chart, knit to 1 st before marker, m1r, K1, sm, K1, m1l, knit to end. (70 sts) Row 27: P30, work Tie Chart, purl to end.
- Row 28: K33, work Tie Chart, knit to end.
- Row 29: As Row 27.

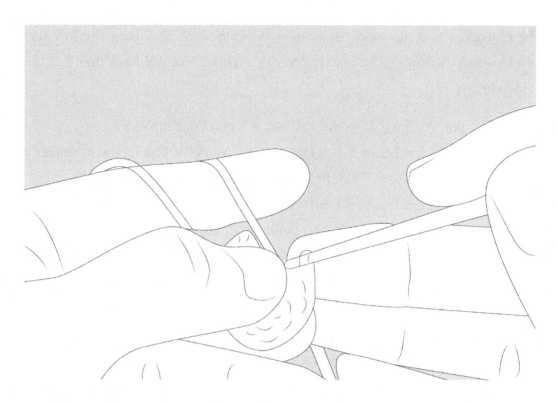

- Row 30: Knit to 1 st before marker, m1r, K1, sm, K1, m1l, K13, work Tie Chart, knit to 1 st before marker, m1r, K1, sm, K1, m1l, knit to end. (74 sts) Row 31: P32, work Tie Chart, purl to end.
- Row 32: K35, work Tie Chart, knit to end.
- Row 33: As Row 31.
- Row 34: Knit to 1 st before marker, m1r, K1, sm, K1, m1l, K14, work Tie Chart, knit to 1 st before marker, m1r, K1, sm, K1, m1l, knit to end. (78 sts) Row 35: P34, work Tie Chart, purl to end.
- Row 36: Knit.
- Row 37: Purl.
- Change to 3mm straight needles.
- Rows 38-41: Knit 4 rows.
- Cast off.

For the Sleeves:

- Starting under the arm, slip the 23 sts held on waste yarn for one sleeve evenly onto three 3.5mm dpns and rejoin the yarn.
- Using the fourth dpn, start knitting in the round.
- Rnd 1: Pick up and knit one stitch from under the arm, knit to end, and pick up and knit one stitch from under the arm. (25 sts) Rnds 2-4: Knit 3 rnds.
- Rnd 5: K1, m1l, knit to last st, m1r, K1. (27 sts) Rnds 6-12: Knit 7 rnds.
- Rnd 13: K1, m1l, knit to last st, m1r, K1. (29 sts) Rnds 14-20: Knit 7 rnds.

- Change to a set of 3mm dpns.
- Rnd 21: Knit.
- Rnd 22: Purl.
- Rnds 23-24: Rpt last two rnds once more.
- Repeat for the second sleeve.

Making Up:

- Close the hole under the arm with several stitches if necessary.
- Block T-shirt.
- Sew buttons on the left-hand button band, matching them up with the buttonholes.

For the Waistcoat:

The waistcoat is worked in one piece from the bottom up, back and forth in rows, and seamed at the shoulders.

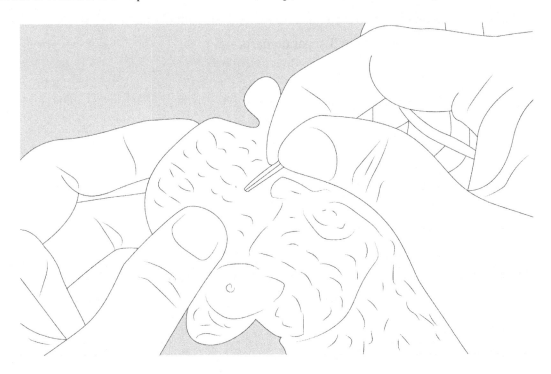

- Using 3mm straight needles and Yarn C, cast on 100 sts.
- Row 1 (ws): Knit.
- Rows 2-3: Knit 2 rows.
- Change to 3.5mm straight needles.
- Row 4 (buttonhole row): K12, CDD, K70, CDD, K9, K2tog, YO, K1. (96 sts) Row 5: K3, P19, K10, P32, K10, P19, K3.
- Row 6: K11, CDD, K68, CDD, K11. (92 sts)
- Row 7: K3, P17, K10, P32, K10, P17, K3.

- Row 8: K10, CDD, K66, CDD, K10. (88 sts)
- Row 9: K3, P15, K5, pm, K5, P32, K5, pm, K5, P15, K3.
- Row 10: K9, CDD, [knit to 2 sts before marker, K2tog, sm, SSK] twice, K9, CDD, K9. (80 sts) Row 11: K3, P3, K7, P3, K8, P32, K8, P3, K7, P3, K3.
- Row 12 (buttonhole row): Knit to last three sts, K2tog, YO, K1.
- Row 13: As Row 11.
- Row 14: [Knit to 2 sts before marker, K2tog, sm, SSK] twice, knit to end. (76 sts) Row 15: K3, P3, K7, P3, K6, P32, K6, P3, K7, P3, K3.
- Row 16: Knit.
- Row 17: K3, P13, K6, P32, K6, P13, K3.
- Row 18: As Row 14. (72 sts)
- Row 19: K3, P10, K10, P26, K10, P10, K3.
- Row 20 (buttonhole row): K16 (right front), cast off four sts, K32 (this includes the st from the last cast off) (back), cast off four sts, K13 (this includes the st from the last cast off), K2tog, YO, K1. (64 sts) The waistcoat is now worked in 3 separate parts.

For the Left Front

- Work over the first 16 sts only.
- Row 21: K3, P10, K3.
- Row 22: K3, SSK, K11. (15 sts)
- Row 23: K3, P9, K3.
- Row 24: K3, SSK, K5, K2tog, K3. (13 sts)
- Row 25: K3, P7, K3.
- Row 26: Knit to last five sts, K2tog, K3. (12 sts) Row 27: K3, purl to last 3 sts, K3.
- Rows 28-37: Rpt Rows 26-27 5 more times. (7 sts) Row 38: K2, K2tog, K3. (6 sts)
- Row 39: Knit.
- Row 40: K1, K2tog, K3. (5 sts)
- Rows 41-43: Knit 3 rows.

Cast off.

For the Back:

- With RS facing, rejoins yarn and work over the next 32 sts only.
- Row 21: K3, purl to last 3 sts, K3.
- Row 22: K3, SSK, knit to last five sts, K2tog, K3. (30 sts) Rows 23-24: Rpt Rows 21-22 once more. (28 sts) Row 25: K3, purl to last 3 sts, K3.

- Row 26: Knit.
- Rows 27-34: Rpt Rows 25-26 4 more times.
- Row 35: K3, P3, K16, P3, K3.
- Row 36: Knit.
- Row 37: K3, P2, K18, P2, K3.
- Row 38: K3, K2tog, K3 (right shoulder), cast off 12 sts, K3 (this includes the st from the last cast off), SSK, K3 (left shoulder). (14 sts) The right and left shoulders are worked separately

For the Left Shoulder:

- Work over the next seven sts only.
- Row 39: Knit.
- Row 40: K2, SSK, K3. (6 sts)
- Row 41: Knit.
- Row 42: K2, SSK, K2. (5 sts)
- Row 43: Knit.
- Cast off.

For the Right Shoulder:

- With WS facing, rejoin yarn and work over the seven sts of the right shoulder.
- Row 39: Knit.
- Row 40: K3, K2tog, K2. (6 sts)
- Row 41: Knit.
- Row 42: K2, K2tog, K2. (5 sts)
- Row 43: Knit.
- Cast off.

For the Right Front:

- With WS facing, rejoin yarn and work over the remaining 16 sts.
- Row 21: K3, P10, K3.
- Row 22: K11, K2tog, K3. (15 sts)
- Row 23: K3, P9, K3.
- Row 24: K3, SSK, K5, K2tog, K3. (13 sts)
- Row 25: K3, P7, K3.
- Row 26: K3, SSK, knit to end. (12 sts)
- Row 27: K3, purl to last 3 sts, K3.

- Rows 28-37: Rpt Rows 26-27 5 more times. (7 sts) Row 38: K3, SSK, K2. (6 sts)
- Row 39: Knit.
- Row 40: K3, SSK, K1. (5 sts)
- Rows 41-43: Knit 3 rows.
- Cast off.

Making Up:

- Block the waistcoat.
- Sew shoulder seams.
- Sew buttons on the right-hand button band, matching them up with the buttonholes.
- Sew a button in the center of each pocket (the garter stitch band just above the central line of decreases on each front).

For the Cable Shorts:

The shorts are worked top down with no seams. The top part is worked back and forth with a button band down the back and some short row shaping for the bottom; the lower half and legs are worked in the round.

- Using 3mm straight needles and Yarn B, cast on 52 sts.
- Row 1 (ws): Knit.
- Row 2: Knit.
- Row 3 (buttonhole row): Knit to last three sts, K2tog, YO, K1.
- Rows 4-5: Knit 2 rows.
- Change to 3.5mm straight needles.
- Row 6: [K1, K1fb] 11 times, K1fb 3 times, K1, K1fb 4 times, [K1, K1fb] 10 times, K2. (80 sts) Row 7: K2, P8, turn.
- Row 8: YO, knit to end.
- Row 9: K2, P8, SSP, P2, turn.
- Row 10: YO, knit to end.
- Row 11: K2, P11, SSP, P2, turn.
- Row 12: YO, knit to end.
- Row 13: K2, P14, SSP, P2, turn.
- Row 14: YO, knit to end.
- Row 15: K2, P17, SSP, purl to last two sts, K2.
- Row 16: K10, turn.
- Row 17: YO, purl to last two sts, K2.
- Row 18: K10, K2tog, K2, turn.

- Row 19 (buttonhole row): YO, purl to last three sts, P2tog, YO, K1.

- Row 20: K13, K2tog, K2, turn.

- Row 21: YO, purl to last two sts, K2.

- Row 22: K16, K2tog, K2, turn.

- Row 23: YO, purl to last two sts, K2.

- Row 24: K19, K2tog, knit to end.

- Row 25: K2, P15, P1fb, P4, P1fb, P3, P1fb, P2, place pattern marker, P23, P1fb, P3, P1fb, P4, P1fb, P2, place pattern marker, P14, K2. (86 sts) Row 26: [Knit to pattern marker, C4F, K8, C4B] twice, knit to end.

- Row 27 (buttonhole row): K2, purl to last three sts, P2tog, YO, K1.

- Row 28: [Knit to pattern marker, K2, C4F, K4, C4B, K2] twice, knit to end.

- Row 29: K2, purl to last two sts, K2.

- Row 30: [Knit to pattern marker, K4, C4F, C4B, K4] twice, knit to end.

- Row 31: K2, purl to last two sts, K2.

- Row 32: Transfer sts to a 3.5mm circular needle, [Knit to pattern marker, C4F, K8, C4B] twice, knit to last two sts, and slip the last two sts (without working them) onto a cable needle.

Join to work in the round:

- Rnd 33: Position the cable needle behind the first two sts on the LH needle, knit the first st on the LH needle together with the first st on the cable needle, place a marker for the beginning of the round, and knit the next st on the LH needle together with the remaining st on the cable needle, knit to end. (84 sts) Rnd 34: [Knit to pattern marker, K2, C4F, K4, C4B, K2] twice, knit to end.

- Rnd 35: Knit.

- Rnd 36: [Knit to pattern marker, K4, C4F, C4B, K4] twice, knit to end.

- Rnd 37: Knit.

- Rnd 38: K1, m1l, [knit to pattern marker, C4F, K8, C4B] twice, knit to last st, m1r, K1. (86 sts) Rnd 39: Knit.

- Rnd 40: [Knit to pattern marker, K2, C4F, K4, C4B, K2] twice, knit to end.

- Rnd 41: K1, m1l, knit to last st, m1r, K1. (88 sts) Rnd 42: Knit to pattern marker, K4, C4F, C4B, K14, m1r, K2, m1l, knit to pattern marker, K4, C4F, C4B, knit to end. (90 sts) Rnd 43: K1, m1l, knit to last st, m1r, K1. (92 sts) Rnd 44: [Knit to pattern marker, C4F, K8, C4B] twice, knit to end.

- Rnd 45: K1, m1l, K44, m1r, K2, m1l, K44, m1r, K1. (96 sts) Rnd 46: [Knit to pattern marker, K2, C4F, K4, C4B, K2] twice, knit to end.

- Rnd 47: K1, m1l, K46, m1r, K2, m1l, K46, m1r, K1. (100 sts) Rnd 48: [Knit to pattern marker, K4, C4F, C4B, K4] twice, knit to end.

Divide for Legs:

- Rnd 49: K50 (right leg), without working them, place the next 50 sts onto waste yarn (left leg).

For the Right Leg:

- Rnd 50: Knit to pattern marker, C4F, K8, C4B, knit to end.
- Rnd 51: Knit.
- Rnd 52: Knit to pattern marker, K2, C4F, K4, C4B, K2, knit to end.
- Rnd 53: Knit.
- Rnd 54: SSK, knit to 2 sts before pattern marker, K2tog, K4, C4F, C4B, K4, knit to end. (48 sts) Rnd 55: Knit.
- Rnds 56-67: Rpt Rnds 50-55 twice more. (44 sts) Rnds 68-71: Rpt Rnds 50-53.
- Rnd 72: Knit to pattern marker, K4, C4F, C4B, K4, knit to end.
- Change to a 3mm circular needle.
- Rnd 73: K14, [SSK, K4, K2tog] twice, knit to end. (40 sts) Rnd 74: Purl.
- Rnd 75: Knit.
- Rnd 76: Purl.
- Cast off.

For the Left Leg:

- Rnd 49: Transfer sts from waste yarn to 3.5mm circular needle, rejoin yarn, and knit one rnd placing marker for beginning of rnd.
- Rnd 50: Knit to pattern marker, C4F, K8, C4B, knit to end.
- Rnd 51: Knit.
- Rnd 52: Knit to pattern marker, K2, C4F, K4, C4B, K2, knit to end.
- Rnd 53: Knit.
- Rnd 54: Knit to pattern marker, K4, C4F, C4B, K4, SSK, knit to last two sts, K2tog. (48 sts) Rnd 55: Knit.
- Rnds 56-67: Rpt Rnds 50-55 twice more. (44 sts)
- Rnds 68-71: Rpt Rnds 50-53.
- Rnds 72-76: Work as Rnds 72-76 of Right Leg.
- Cast off.

Making Up:

- If necessary, close the hole where the two legs join with a couple of stitches.
- Block shorts.

- Sew buttons in place on the left-hand button band down the back of the pants, matching them up with the buttonholes.

For the T-Bar Shoes:

- Using 2.75mm needles and Yarn A for the soles, follow the pattern for the T-Bar Shoe, changing to Yarn C for the upper part of the shoes.

2. Hedgehog

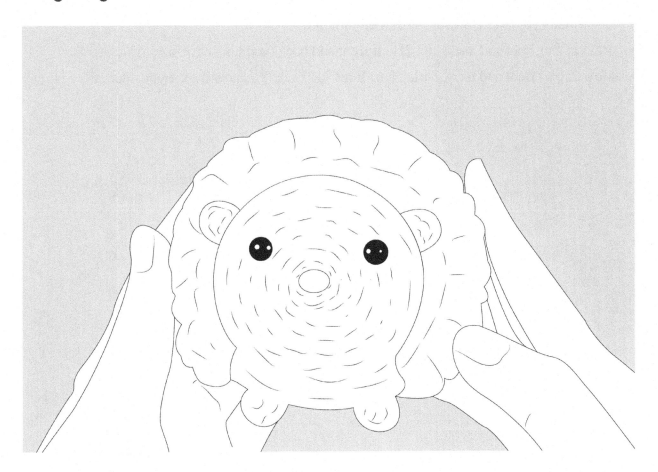

Materials:

- Size 5 needles
- 80 yds yarn

Gauge:

- Irrelevant as this is not being worn

Size:

- Roughly 4 inches long

Instructions:

For the Ears (Make 2):

- Cast off eight stockinette stitches in contrasting colors, join in the round
- Round 1: knit into the front and back of 16 stitches
- Knit every round till it measures about 1/2 inches, then cast off weave in the top end and attach to the hedgehog.

For the Back of the Body:

- In the main color, cast off four stockinette stitches
- Row 1: knit front and back, knit 2, knit front and back (you now have six stitches.)
- Row 2: purl front and back, purl 4, purl front and back (you now have eight stitches)

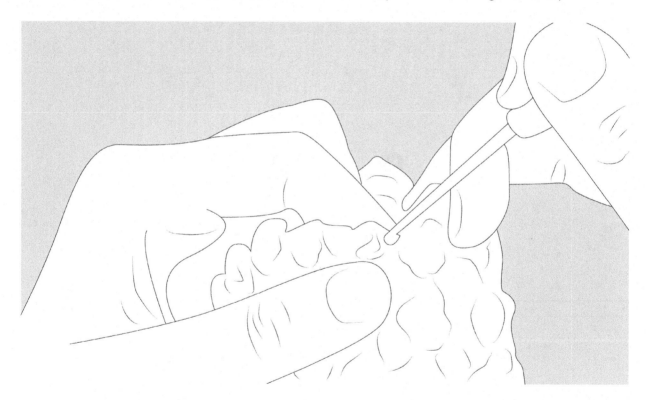

- Row 3: knit front and back, knit 6, knit front and back (you now have ten stitches)
- Row 4: purl front and back, purl 8, purl front and back (you now have 12 stitches)
- Work in stockinette stitch for about ten rows 2 inches from cast on, end after a purl row.
- Decreasing
- Row 1: slip, slip, knit, knit eight stitches, knit two together (you now have ten stitches)
- Row 2: purl two together, purl six stitches, and purl two together (you now have eight stitches)
- Row 3: slip, slip, knit, knit 4, knit two together (you now have six stitches)
- Row 4: purl two together, P2, purl two together (you now have four stitches)

For the Body:

Continued from the back of the body

- Knit the four stockinette stitches on the needle. On the same needle, pick up 10 stockinette stitches around the back of the body, continuing around till there are 42 stockinette stitches, 14 per needle
- Round 1: Knit front and back, knit to the last stockinette stitch on the needle,

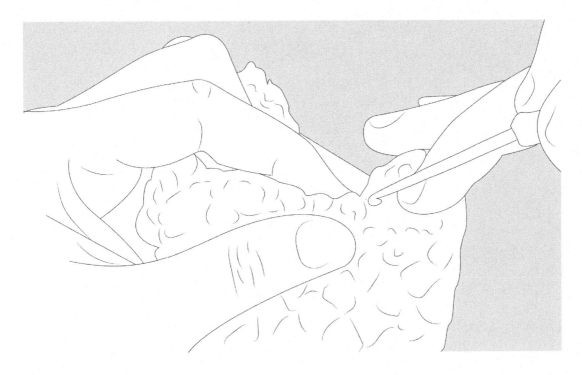

- and knit through front and back; repeat for each needle: 16 stockinette stitches per needle (48)
- Repeat Round 1, then 18 stockinette stitches per needle (You now have 54 stitches total)
- Knit every round alternating between pulled curl stitch and knit around till about 1 1/2 inches long. Try one pulled curl stitch round and two knit rounds for less work. It doesn't create as full of a look.
- Find out where your hedgehog's belly is, and always knit that needle.
- Create a curled stitch; knit into a stockinette stitch, tug it out 2 inches, twist around your finger, and then put it back onto your needle. Knit normal and curled stitch together.

Decreasing Rounds:

- Continue alternating between normal knit and curled stitches
- Round 1: Knit 7, knit two together, then repeat 16 stockinette stitches per needle (You now have 48 stitches total)
- Rounds 2-5: Knit all (4 rounds total)
- Round 6: Knit 6, knit two together, then repeat 14 stockinette stitches per needle (you now have 42 stitches total)

- Round 7: Knit 5, knit two together, then repeat 12 stockinette stitches per needle (you now have 36 stitches total)
- Round 8: Knit all

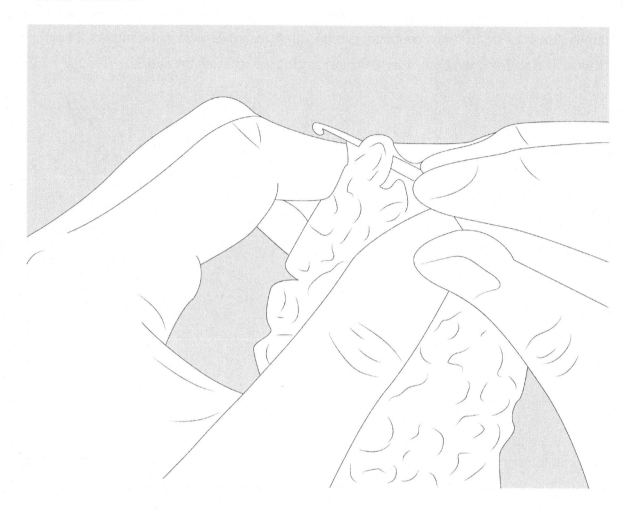

- Round 9: Knit 4, knit two together, ten stockinette stitches per needle (you now have 30 stitches total)
- Round 10: Knit all (end on the curled round)
- Round 11: Switch to contrasting colors and stop curl stitches. Knit all
- Round 12: Knit 2 together, knit to last two stockinette stitches on the needle, knit two together, and repeat eight stockinette stitches per needle (you now have 24 stitches total)
- Round 13-17: knit all (5 rounds). Begin stuffing as you go
- Round 18: Knit 2 together, knit to last two stockinette stitches on the needle, knit two together, and repeat six stockinette stitches per needle (you now have 18 stitches total)
- Round 19-21: knit all (3 rounds)
- Round 22: Knit 2 together, knit to last two stockinette stitches on the needle, knit two together, and repeat four stockinette stitches per needle (you now have 12 stitches total)
- Round 23: Knit all

- Round 24: Knit 2 together, two stockinette stitches per needle (you now have six stitches total)
- Finish stuffing. Cut the yarn, leaving a long tail. Pull the end through the remaining stockinette stitches, gather up tight to close the hole, and stitch to secure. Weave your leftover yarn to the inside.

3. Raccoon

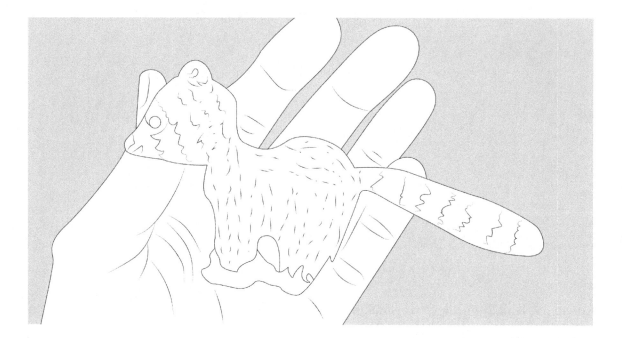

Materials:

For the Body:

- Scheepjes Stonewashed (50g/130m; 78% cotton/22% acrylic) yarn in the following shades:
  - Yarn A Grey (Smokey Quartz 802), two balls
  - Yarn B Cream (Moonstone 801), one ball
  - Yarn C Black (Black Onyx 803), one ball
- 2.75mm (US 2) straight needles
- Toy stuffing
- 2 x 10mm (1â□„2in) buttons
- Scrap piece of 4-ply yarn for embroidering the nose

For the Outfit:

- Scheepjes Catona (10g/25m, 25g/62m, or 50g/125m; 100% cotton) yarn in the following shades:
  - Yarn A Red (Candy Apple 516), 1 x 50g ball
  - Yarn B Dark Blue (Light Navy 164), 1 x 25g ball
  - Yarn C Cream (Old Lace 130), 1 x 25g ball
- 2.75mm (US 2) straight needles
- 3mm (US 21â□„2) straight needles
- 3mm (US 21â□„2) circular needle (23cm/9in length)
- Set of four 3mm (US 21â□„2) double-pointed needles

- 3.5mm (US 4) straight needles
- 3.5mm (US 4) circular needle (23cm/9in length)
- Set of four 3.5mm (US 4) double-pointed needles
- Cable needle
- Waste yarn
- Six small buttons

Before you start, read the Essential Notes at the beginning of this book.

Instructions for the Raccoon:

For the Head:

Starting at the neck:

- Using Yarn A and 2.75mm straight needles, cast on 11 sts.
- Row 1 (ws): (A) P4, (B) P3, (A) P4.
- Row 2: (A) [K1, M1] 4 times, (B) [K1, M1] 3 times, (A) [K1, M1] 3 times, K1. (21 sts) Row 3: (A) P7, (B) P6, (A) P8.

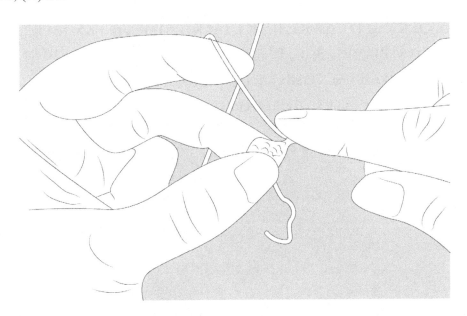

- Row 4: (A) [K2, M1] 3 times, K2, (B) [M1, K2] 3 times, (A) [M1, K2] 3 times, M1, K1. (31 sts) Row 5: (A) P11, (B) P9, (A) P11.
- Row 6: (A) K1, m1l, K10, (B) K9, (A) K10, m1r, K1. (33 sts) Row 7: (A) P12, (B) P9, (A) P12.
- Row 8: (A) K1, m1l, K10, (B) K5, m1r, K1, m1l, K5, (A) K10, m1r, K1. (37 sts) Row 9: (A) P12, (B) P13, (A) P12.
- Row 10: (A) K1, m1l, K10, (B) K7, m1r, K1, m1l, K7, (A) K10, m1r, K1. (41 sts) Row 11: (A) P12, (B) P8, m1pl, P1, m1pr, P8, (A) P12. (43 sts) Row 12: (A) K1, m1l, K10, (B) K10, m1r, K1, m1l,

K10, (A) K10, m1r, K1. (47 sts) Row 13: (A) P12, (B) P11, m1pl, P1, m1pr, P11, (A) P12. (49 sts) Row 14: (A) K11, (B) K13, m1r, K1, m1l, K13, (A) K11. (51 sts) Row 15: (A) P11, (B) P14, m1pl, P1, m1pr, P14, (A) P11. (53 sts) Row 16: (A) K1, m1l, K9, (B) K16, m1r, K1, m1l, K16, (A) K9, m1r, K1. (57 sts) Row 17: (A) P11, (B) P35, (A) P11.

- Row 18: (A) K10, (B) K4, (C) K6, (B) K8, m1r, K1, m1l, K8, (C) K6, (B) K4, (A) K10. (59 sts) Row 19: (A) P10, (B) P3, (C) P7, (B) P19, (C) P7, (B) P3, (A) P10.

- Row 20: (A) K9, (B) K3, (C) K8, (B) K9, sl1, K9, (C) K8, (B) K3, (A) K9.

- Row 21: (A) P9, (B) P2, (C) P9, (B) P19, (C) P9, (B) P2, (A) P9.

- Row 22: (A) K8, (B) K2, (C) K11, (B) K7, CDD, K7, (C) K11, (B) K2, (A) K8. (57 sts) Row 23: (A) P8, (B) P2, (C) P11, (B) P15, (C) P11, (B) P2, (A) P8.

- Row 24: (A) K9, (B) K2, (C) K10, (B) K6, CDD, K6, (C) K10, (B) K2, (A) K9. (55 sts) Row 25: (A) P9, (B) P2, (C) P11, (B) P4, PCDD, P4, (C) P11, (B) P2, (A) P9. (53 sts) Row 26: (A) K10, (B) K2, (C) K10, (B) K3, CDD, K3, (C) K10, (B) K2, (A) K10. (51 sts) Row 27: (A) P10, (B) P2, (C) P11, (B) P1, PCDD, P1, (C) P11, (B) P2, (A) P10. (49 sts) Row 28: (A) K1, K2tog, K8, (B) K2, (C) K10, CDD, K10, (B) K2, (A) K8, SSK, K1. (45 sts) Row 29: (A) P10, (B) P2, (C) P9, PCDD, P9, (B) P2, (A) P10. (43 sts) Row 30: (A) K11, (B) K2, (C) K7, CDD, K7, (B) K2, (A) K11. (41 sts) Row 31: (A) P11, (B) P2, (C) P6, (A) P3, (C) P6, (B) P2, (A) P11.

- Row 32: (A) K1, K2tog, K9, (B) K2, (C) K5, (A) K1, sl1, K1, (C) K5, (B) K2, (A) K9, SSK, K1. (39 sts) Row 33: (A) P11, (B) P3, (C) P3, (B) P1, (A) P3, (B) P1, (C) P3, (B) P3, (A) P11.

- Row 34: (A) K12, (B) K6, (A) K1, sl1, K1, (B) K6, (A) K12.

- Row 35: (A) P12, (B) P6, (A) P3, (B) P6, (A) P12.

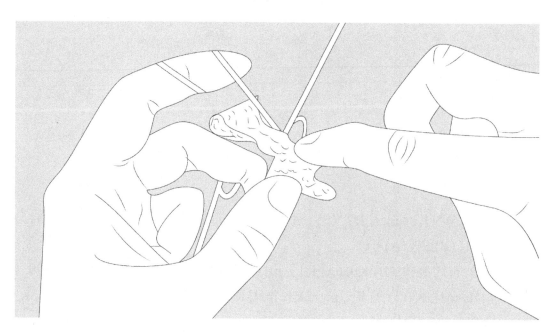

- Row 36: (A) K1, K2tog, K10, (B) K5, (A) K1, sl1, K1, (B) K5, (A) K10, SSK, K1. (37 sts) Row 37: (A) P13, (B) P3, (A) P5, (B) P3, (A) P13.

Continue in Yarn A only.

- Row 38: K18, sl1, K18.
- Row 39: Purl.
- Row 40: K1, K2tog, K3, K2tog 4 times, K3, CDD, K3, SSK 4 times, K3, SSK, K1. (25 sts) Row 41: Purl.
- Row 42: K1, K2tog 5 times, CDD, SSK 5 times, K1. (13 sts) Row 43: Purl.
- Cast off.

For the Ears (Make 2):

- Using 2.75mm straight needles and Yarn A, cast on 18 sts.
- Row 1 (ws): (A) P7, (C) P4, (A) P7.
- Row 2: (A) K7, (C) [K1, M1] 3 times, K1, (A) K7. (21 sts) Row 3: (A) P7, (C) P7, (A) P7.
- Row 4: (A) K7, (C) K7, (A) K7.
- Row 5: (A) P7, (C) P7, (A) P7.
- Row 6: (A) K4, K2tog, K1, (C) SSK, K3, K2tog, (A) K1, SSK, K4. (17 sts) Row 7: (A) P6, (C) P5, (A) P6.
- Row 8: (A) K6, (C) K5, (A) K6.
- Row 9: (A) P6, (C) P5, (A) P6.

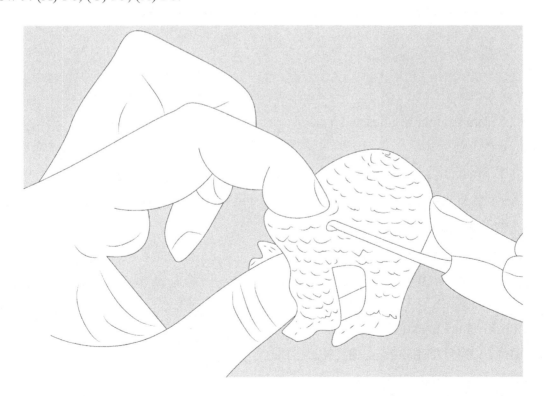

- Row 10: (A) K3, K2tog, K1, (C) SSK, K1, K2tog, (A) K1, SSK, K3. (13 sts) Row 11: (A) P5, (C) P3, (A) P5.

Continue in Yarn A only.

- Row 12: K2, K2tog, SSK, K1, K2tog, SSK, K2. (9 sts) Row 13: Purl.
- Row 14: K1, K2tog, sl1 kw, K2tog, PSSO, SSK, K1. (5 sts) Cut yarn, leaving a long tail. Using a tapestry needle, thread the tail through the stitches left on the needle and pull up tight to gather stitches.

For the Tail:

- Using 2.75mm straight needles and Yarn A, cast on 19 sts.
- Row 1 (ws): Purl.
- Rows 2-3: Stocking stitch two rows.
- Work rows 4-35 in a stripe rpt of 4 rows Yarn C and four rows Yarn A, starting with Yarn C.
- Rows 4-5: Stocking stitch two rows.
- Row 6: K4, [M1, K6] twice, M1, K3. (22 sts)
- Rows 7-9: Stocking stitch three rows.
- Row 10: K1, [M1, K7] 3 times. (25 sts)
- Rows 11-13: Stocking stitch three rows.
- Row 14: K3, [M1, K4] 5 times, M1, K2. (31 sts)
- Rows 15-33: Stocking stitch 19 rows.
- Row 34: K6, SSK, K1, K2tog, K20. (29 sts)
- Row 35: Purl.

Continue in Yarn C only.

- Row 36: K19, SSK, K1, K2tog, K5. (27 sts)
- Row 37: Purl.
- Row 38: K5, SSK, K1, K2tog, K17. (25 sts)
- Row 39: Purl.
- Row 40: [K4, SSK, K1, K2tog, K3] twice, K1. (21 sts) Row 41: Purl.
- Row 42: [K3, SSK, K1, K2tog, K2] twice, K1. (17 sts) Row 43: Purl.
- Row 44: [K2, SSK, K1, K2tog, K1] twice, K1. (13 sts) Row 45: Purl.
- Row 46: [K1, SSK, K1, K2tog] twice, K1. (9 sts)
- Row 47: Purl.
- Row 48: SSK, K1, K2tog, CDD, K1. (5 sts)
- Row 49: Purl.
- Cut yarn, leaving a long tail. Using a tapestry needle, thread the tail through the stitches left on the needle and pull up tight to gather stitches.

For the Body:

- Work as Standard Body - Chest Blaze.

For the Arms (Make 2):

- Work as Standard Arms .

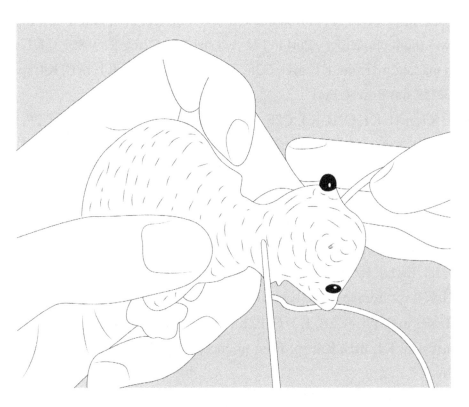

For the Legs (Make 2):

- Work as Standard Leg - Contrast Foot Pad, but using Yarn C instead of Yarn B for Rows 1-8.

Making Up:

- Follow the instructions in the techniques section.

Instructions for the Outfit:

For the Diamond Sweater:

The sweater is worked top down, with raglan sleeves and no seams. The top half is worked back and forth in rows with a button band opening, and the body and sleeves are worked in the round.

Note the following special abbreviations:

'C2B' - Place 1 st on CN, hold to back, slip 1 st purlwise wyib, knit st from CN.

'C2F' - Place 1 st on CN, hold to front, K1, slip 1 st purlwise wyib from CN.

Using Yarn A and 3.5mm straight needles, cast on 36 sts.

- Row 1 (ws): Purl.
- Rows 2-4: Stocking stitch three rows.
- Row 5: Cast on three sts using Purl cast-on method, P5, P1fb, P3, pm, P6, P1fb, P5, pm, P2, P1fb, P3, pm, P3, P1fb, purl to end. (43 sts) Row 6: P3, K1, m1l, K1, C2B, C2F, [knit to marker, m1r, sm, K1, m1l] twice, K4, C2B, C2F, knit to marker, m1r, sm, K1, m1l, knit to last four sts, m1r, K1, P3. (51 sts) Row 7 (buttonhole row): Purl to last two sts, YO, P2tog Row 8: P3, K1, m1l, K1, C2B, K2, C2F, knit to marker, m1r, sm, K1, m1l, C2F, K4, C2B, m1r, sm, K1, m1l, K4; rpt from to once, K5, m1r, K1, P3. (59 sts) Row 9: Purl.
- Row 10: P3, K1, m1l, K1, C2B, K4, C2F, K2, C2B, m1r, sm, K1, m1l, K2, C2F, K2, C2B, K2, m1r, sm, K1, m1l, C2F, K2; rpt from to once, K1, m1r, K1, P3. (67 sts) Row 11: Purl.
- Row 12: P3, K1, m1l, K1, C2B, K6, C2F, C2B, K2, m1r, sm, K1, m1l, K4, C2F, C2B, K4, m1r, sm, K1, m1l, K2, C2F; rpt from to once, K3, m1r, K1, P3. (75 sts) Row 13 (buttonhole row): As Row 7.
- Row 14: P3, K1, m1l, K1, C2B, K8, C2B, K4, m1r, sm, K1, m1l, K6, C2B, K6, m1r, sm, K1, m1l, K4; rpt from to once, K5, m1r, K1, P3. (83 sts) Row 15: Purl.
- Row 16: P3, K1, m1l, K1, C2B, C2F, K6, C2B, C2F, K4, m1r, sm, K1, m1l, K6, C2B, C2F, K6, m1r, sm, K1, m1l, K4; rpt from to once, K5, m1r, K1, P3. (91 sts) Row 17: Purl.
- Row 18: P3, K1, m1l, K1, [C2B, K2, C2F, K4] twice, m1r, sm, K1, m1l, C2F, K4, C2B, K2, C2F, K4, C2B, m1r, sm, K1, m1l, K4; rpt from to once, K5, m1r, K1, P3. (99 sts) Row 19 (buttonhole row): As Row 7.

- Row 20: P3, K1, m1l, K1, [C2B, K4, C2F, K2] twice, C2B, m1r, sm, K1, m1l, K2, C2F, K2, C2B, K4, C2F, K2, C2B, K2, m1r, sm, K1, m1l, C2F, K2; rpt from to once, K1, m1r, K1, P3. (107 sts) Row 21: Purl.

- Row 22: P3, K1, m1l, K1, [C2B, K6, C2F] twice, C2B, K2, m1r, sm, K1, m1l, K4, C2F, C2B, K6, C2F, C2B, K4, m1r, sm, K1, m1l, K2, C2F; rpt from to once, K3, m1r, K1, P3. (115 sts) Row 23: Purl.

- Row 24: Transfer sts to a 3.5mm circular needle, P3, K1, m1l, K1, [C2B, K8] twice, C2B, K4, m1r, sm, K1, m1l, K6, C2B, K8, C2B, K6, m1r, sm, K1, m1l, K4; rpt from to once, K5, m1r, K1, slip the last three sts (without working them) onto a cable needle. (123 sts) Join to work in the round:

- Rnd 25: Position cable needle behind first three sts on LH needle, place marker for beginning of the round, knit first st on LH needle together with first st on cable needle; rpt for next two sts, knit to marker, sm, K1 (back), without working them place next 26 sts onto waste yarn (sleeve), remove marker; rpt from to once (front and sleeve). (68 sts) Rnd 26: K1, m1l, K4, C2B, [C2F, K6, C2B] twice, C2F, knit to marker, m1r, sm, K2, m1l; rpt from to once, knit to last st, m1r, K1. (72 sts) Rnd 27: Knit.

- Rnd 28: K5, [C2B, K2, C2F, K4] 3 times, K1; rpt from once more.

- Rnd 29: Knit.

- Rnd 30: K1, m1l, K3, [C2B, K4, C2F, K2] twice, C2B, K4, C2F, knit to marker, m1r, sm, K2, m1l; rpt from to once, knit to last st, m1r, K1. (76 sts) Rnd 31: Knit.

- Rnd 32: K2, [C2F, C2B, K6] 3 times, C2F, C2B, K2; rpt from once more.

- Rnd 33: Knit.

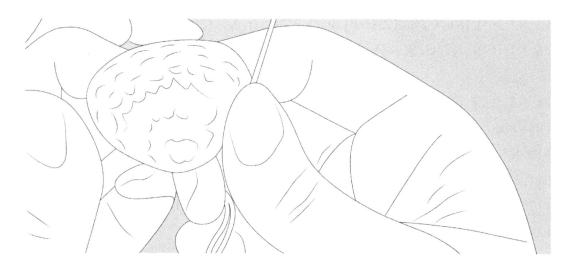

- Rnd 34: K1, m1l, K2, [C2B, K8] 3 times, C2B, knit to marker, m1r, sm, K2, m1l; rpt from to once, knit to last st, m1r, K1. (80 sts) Rnd 35: Knit.

- Rnd 36: K3, [C2B, C2F, K6] 7 times, C2B, C2F, K3.

- Rnd 37: Knit.

- Rnd 38: K1, m1l, K1, [C2B, K2, C2F, K4] 3 times, C2B, K2, C2F, K1, m1r, sm, K2, m1l; rpt from to once, K1, m1r, K1. (84 sts) Rnd 39: Knit.
- Rnd 40: K2, [C2B, K4, C2F, K2] 8 times, K2.
- Rnd 41: Knit.
- Rnd 42: K1, [C2B, K6, C2F] 4 times, K1; rpt from once more.
- Rnd 43: Knit.
- Rnd 44: [C2B, K8] 4 times, C2F; rpt from once more.
- Change to a 3mm circular needle.
- Rnd 45: K19, K2tog, K40, K2tog, K21. (82 sts)
- Rnd 46: Purl.
- Rnd 47: Knit.
- Rnd 48: Purl.
- Cast off.

For the Sleeves:

- Starting under the arm, slip the 26 sts held on waste yarn for one sleeve evenly onto three 3.5mm dpns and rejoin the yarn.
- Using the fourth dpn, start knitting in the round.
- Rnd 1: Knit.
- Rnd 2: [K6, C2B, C2F] twice, K6.
- Rnd 3: Knit.
- Rnd 4: K1, m1l, [K4, C2B, K2, C2F] twice, K4, m1r, K1. (28 sts) Rnd 5: Knit.
- Rnd 6: K1, [C2F, K2, C2B, K4] twice, C2F, K2, C2B, K1.
- Rnd 7: Knit.
- Rnd 8: K2, [C2F, C2B, K6] twice, C2F, C2B, K2.
- Rnd 9: Knit.
- Rnd 10: K3, [C2B, K8] twice, C2B, K3.
- Rnd 11: Knit.
- Rnd 12: K1, m1l, K1, [C2B, C2F, K6] twice, C2B, C2F, K1, m1r, K1. (30 sts) Rnd 13: Knit.
- Rnd 14: [K2, C2B, K2, C2F, K2] 3 times.
- Rnd 15: Knit.
- Rnd 16: [K1, C2B, K4, C2F, K1] 3 times.
- Rnd 17: Knit.
- Rnd 18: [C2B, K6, C2F] 3 times.
- Rnd 19: Knit.

- Rnd 20: K9, [C2B, K8] twice, K1.
- Change to a set of 3mm dpns.
- Rnd 21: K14, K2tog, K14. (29 sts)
- Rnd 22: Purl.
- Rnd 23: Knit.
- Rnd 24: Purl.

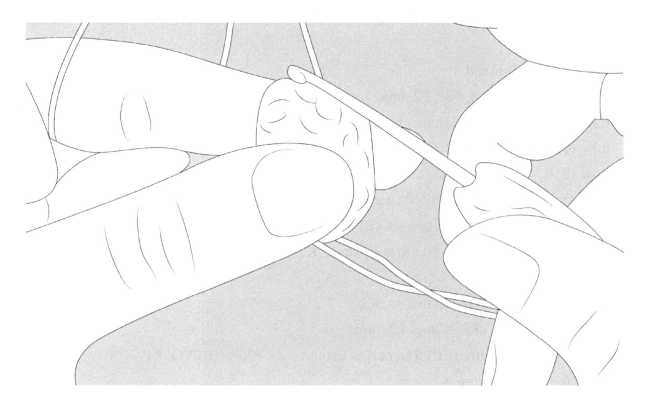

- Cast off.
- Repeat for the second sleeve.

Making Up:

- Close the hole under the arm with several stitches if necessary.
- Block the sweater.
- Sew buttons on the left-hand button band, matching them up with the buttonholes.

For the Striped Shorts:

The shorts are worked top down with no seams. The top part is worked back and forth with a button band opening at the back and some short row shaping for the bottom; the lower half and legs are worked in the round. The button band is worked in Yarn B using the Intarsia method (see Techniques: Colorwork).

- Using 3mm straight needles and Yarn B, cast on 52 sts.
- Row 1 (ws): Knit.
- Row 2: Knit.
- Row 3 (buttonhole row): Knit to last three sts, K2tog, YO, K1.
- Rows 4-5: Knit 2 rows.
- Change to 3.5mm straight needles.
- Row 6: [K1, K1fb] 11 times, K1fb 3 times, K1, K1fb 4 times, [K1, K1fb] 10 times, K2. (80 sts) Row 7: K2, P8, turn.
- Row 8: YO, knit to end.
- Row 9: (B) K2, (C) P8, SSP, P2, turn.
- Row 10: (C) YO, knit to last two sts, (B) K2.
- Row 11: (B) K2, P11, SSP, P2, turn.
- Row 12: (B) YO, knit to end.
- Row 13: (B) K2, (C) P14, SSP, P2, turn.
- Row 14: (C) YO, knit to last two sts, (B) K2.
- Row 15: (B) K2, P17, SSP, purl to last two sts, K2.
- Row 16: (B) K10, turn.
- Row 17: (B) YO, purl to last two sts, K2.
- Row 18: (B) K2, (C) K8, K2tog, K2, turn.
- Row 19 (buttonhole row): (C) YO, purl to last three sts, P2tog, (B) YO, K1.
- Row 20: (B) K13, K2tog, K2, turn.
- Row 21: (B) YO, purl to last two sts, K2.
- Row 22: (B) K2, (C) K14, K2tog, K2, turn.
- Row 23: (C) YO, purl to last two sts, (B) K2.
- Row 24: (B) K19, K2tog, knit to end.
- Row 25: (B) K2, purl to last two sts, K2.
- Row 26: (B) K2, (C) knit to last two sts, (B) K2.
- Row 27 (buttonhole row): (B) K2, (C) purl to last three sts, P2tog, (B) YO, K1.
- Row 28: (B) Knit.
- Row 29: (B) K2, purl to last two sts, K2.
- Row 30: (B) K2, (C) knit to last two sts, (B) K2.
- Row 31: (B) K2, (C) purl to last two sts, (B) K2.
- From this point, the shorts are worked in a stripe pattern of 2 rows of Yarn B and two rows of Yarn C, beginning with Yarn B and without the button band.

- Row 32: Transfer sts to a 3.5mm circular needle and knit to the last two sts; slip the last two sts (without working them) onto a cable needle.

Join to work in the round:

- Rnd 33: Position the cable needle behind the first two sts on the LH needle, knit the first st on the LH needle together with the first st on the cable needle, place marker for beginning of the round, knit the next st on the LH needle together with the remaining st on the cable needle, knit to end. (78 sts) Rnds 34-37: Knit 4 rnds.
- Rnd 38: K1, m1l, knit to last st, m1r, K1. (80 sts) Rnds 39-40: Knit 2 rnds.
- Rnd 41: K1, m1l, knit to last st, m1r, K1. (82 sts) Rnd 42: K40, m1r, K2, m1l, knit to end. (84 sts)
- Rnd 43: K1, m1l, knit to last st, m1r, K1. (86 sts) Rnd 44: Knit.
- Rnd 45: K1, m1l, K41, m1r, K2, m1l, K41, m1r, K1. (90 sts) Rnd 46: Knit.
- Rnd 47: K1, m1l, K43, m1r, K2, m1l, K43, m1r, K1. (94 sts) Rnd 48: Knit.

Divide for Legs:

- Rnd 49: Without working them, K47 (right leg), place the next 47 sts onto waste yarn (left leg).

For the Right Leg:

- Rnds 50-53: Knit 4 rnds.
- Rnd 54: SSK, K22, K2tog, knit to end. (45 sts)
- Rnds 55-57: Knit 3 rnds.
- Rnd 58: SSK, K20, K2tog, knit to end. (43 sts)
- Rnds 59-61: Knit 3 rnds.
- Rnd 62: SSK, K18, K2tog, knit to end. (41 sts)
- Rnd 63: Knit.
- Change to a 3mm circular needle and continue in Yarn B only.
- Rnd 64: Knit.
- Rnd 65: Purl.
- Rnds 66-67: Rpt last two rnds once more.

For the Left Leg:

- Rnd 49: Transfer sts from waste yarn to 3.5mm circular needle, place marker for beginning of the round, and rejoin Yarn B, knit one rnd.
- Continue working on the stripe pattern of 2 rows of Yarn B and two rows of Yarn C, beginning with Yarn C.

- Rnds 50-53: Knit 4 rnds.
- Rnd 54: K21, SSK, K22, K2tog. (45 sts)
- Rnds 55-57: Knit 3 rnds.
- Rnd 58: K21, SSK, K20, K2tog. (43 sts)
- Rnds 59-61: Knit 3 rnds.
- Rnd 62: K21, SSK, K18, K2tog. (41 sts)
- Rnd 63: Knit.
- Change to a 3mm circular needle and continue in Yarn B only.
- Rnd 64: Knit.
- Rnd 65: Purl.
- Rnds 66-67: Rpt last two rnds once more.
- Cast off.

Making Up:

- If necessary, close the hole where the two legs join with a couple of stitches.
- Block the shorts.
- Sew buttons in place on the left-hand button band down the back of the shorts, matching them up with the buttonholes.

For the Sneakers:

- Using 2.75mm needles and Yarn C for the soles, follow the pattern for the Sneakers, changing to Yarn A for the upper parts of the shoes. Make the laces with Yarn C.

4. Hare

Materials:

For the Body:

- Scheepjes Stonewashed (50g/130m; 78% cotton/22% acrylic) yarn in the following shades:
    - Yarn A Ecru (Axinite 831), two balls
    - Yarn B Cream (Moonstone 801), one ball
- 2.75mm (US 2) straight needles
- Toy stuffing
- 2 x 10mm (1.2in) buttons
- Scrap piece of 4-ply yarn for embroidering the nose
- 35mm (13.8in) pompom maker

For the Outfit:

- Scheepjes Catona (10g/25m, 25g/62m, or 50g/125m; 100% cotton) yarn in the following shades:
    - Yarn A Cream (Old Lace 130), 1 x 50g ball, and 1 x 25g ball
    - Yarn B Pale Grey (Light Silver 172), 1 x 50g ball
    - Yarn C Peach (Rich Coral 410), 1 x 10g ball
    - Yarn D Orange (Royal Orange 189), 1 x 10g ball
    - Yarn E Green (Lime 512), 1 x 10g ball

- 3mm (US 2) straight needles
- 3mm (US 2) circular needle (23cm/9in length)
- Set of four 3mm (US 2) double-pointed needles
- 3.5mm (US 4) straight needles
- 3.5mm (US 4) circular needle (23cm/9in length)
- Set of four 3.5mm (US 4) double-pointed needles
- Cable needle
- Waste yarn
- Ten small buttons

Before you start, read the Essential Notes at the beginning of this book.

Instructions for the Hare:

For the Head:

Starting at the neck:

- Using 2.75mm straight needles and Yarn A, cast on 11 sts.
- Row 1 (ws): Purl.

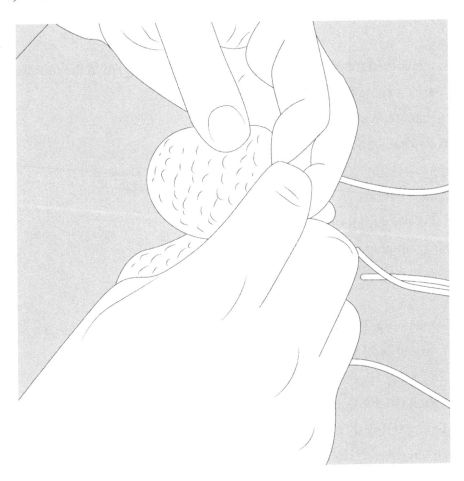

- Row 2: [K1, M1] to last st, K1. (21 sts)

- Row 3: Purl.

- Row 4: [K2, M1] to last st, K1. (31 sts)

- Row 5: Purl.

- Row 6: K1, m1l, knit to last st, m1r, K1. (33 sts) Row 7: Purl.

- Row 8: [K1, m1l, K15, m1r] twice, K1. (37 sts)

- Row 9: Purl.

- Row 10: [K1, m1l, K17, m1r] twice, K1. (41 sts)

- Row 11: P20, m1pl, P1, m1pr, P20. (43 sts)

- Row 12: [K1, m1l, K20, m1r] twice, K1. (47 sts)

- Row 13: P23, m1pl, P1, m1pr, P23. (49 sts)

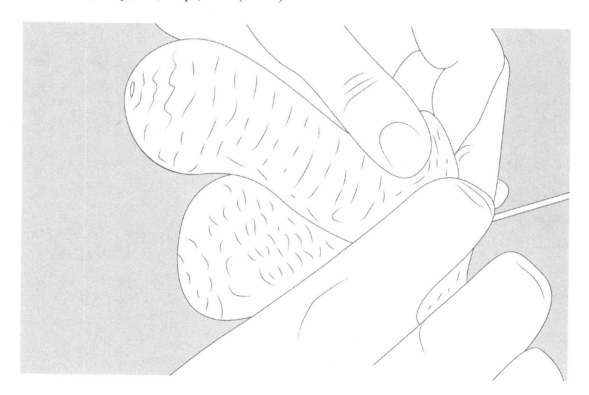

- Row 14: K24, m1r, K1, m1l, K24. (51 sts)

- Row 15: Purl.

- Row 16: [K1, m1l, K24, m1r] twice, K1. (55 sts)

- Row 17: Purl.

- Row 18: K27, sl1, K27.

- Rows 19-21: Rpt last two rows once more, then rpt Row 17 again.

- Row 22: K26, CDD, K26. (53 sts)

- Row 23: Purl.

- Row 24: K25, CDD, K25. (51 sts)

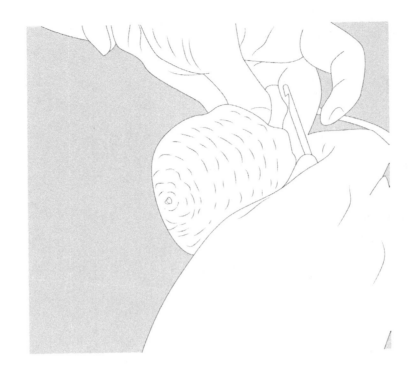

- Row 25: P24, PCDD, P24. (49 sts)

- Row 26: K23, CDD, K23. (47 sts)

- Row 27: Purl.

- Row 28: K1, K2tog, K19, CDD, K19, SSK, K1. (43 sts) Row 29: Purl.

- Row 30: K20, CDD, K20. (41 sts)

- Row 31: Purl.

- Row 32: K1, K2tog, K17, sl1, K17, SSK, K1. (39 sts) Row 33: Purl.

- Row 34: K19, sl1, K19.

- Row 35: Purl.

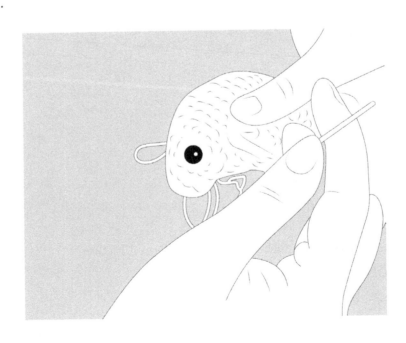

- Row 36: K1, K2tog, K16, sl1, K16, SSK, K1. (37 sts) Row 37: Purl.
- Row 38: K18, sl1, K18.
- Row 39: Purl.
- Row 40: K1, K2tog, K3, K2tog 4 times, K3, CDD, K3, SSK 4 times, K3, SSK, K1. (25 sts) Row 41: Purl.
- Row 42: K1, K2tog 5 times, CDD, SSK 5 times, K1. (13 sts) Row 43: Purl.
- Cast off.

For the Ears (Make 2):

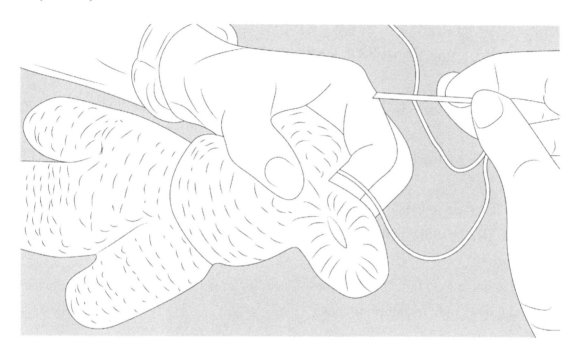

- Using 2.75mm straight needles and Yarn A, cast on 15 sts.
- Row 1 (ws): (A) P6, (B) P3, (A) P6.
- Row 2: (A) K6, (B) [K1, M1] 3 times, (A) K6. (18 sts) Row 3: (A) P6, (B) P6, (A) P6.
- Row 4: (A) K6, (B) K6, (A) K6.
- Row 5: (A) P6, (B) P6, (A) P6.
- Row 6: (A) K4, m1r, K2, (B) K1, m1l, K4, m1r, K1, (A) K2, m1l, K4. (22 sts) Row 7: (A) P7, (B) P8, (A) P7.
- Row 8: (A) K7, (B) K8, (A) K7.
- Row 9: (A) P7, (B) P8, (A) P7.
- Row 10: (A) K5, m1r, K2, (B) K1, m1l, K6, m1r, K1, (A) K2, m1l, K5. (26 sts) Row 11: (A) P8, (B) P10, (A) P8.
- Row 12: (A) K8, (B) K10, (A) K8.
- Rows 13-15: Rpt last two rows once more, then rpt Row 11 again.

- Row 16: (A) K6, m1r, K2, (B) K1, m1l, K8, m1r, K1, (A) K2, m1l, K6. (30 sts) Row 17: (A) P9, (B) P12, (A) P9.
- Row 18: (A) K9, (B) K12, (A) K9.
- Rows 19-27: Rpt last two rows four more times, then rpt Row 17 again.
- Row 28: (A) K6, K2tog, K1, (B) SSK, K8, K2tog, (A) K1, SSK, K6. (26 sts) Row 29: (A) P8, (B) P10, (A) P8.
- Row 30: (A) K8, (B) K10, (A) K8.
- Row 31: (A) P8, (B) P10, (A) P8.
- Row 32: (A) K5, K2tog, K1, (B) SSK, K6, K2tog, (A) K1, SSK, K5. (22 sts) Rows 33-35: Rpt Rows 7-9.
- Row 36: (A) K4, K2tog, K1, (B) SSK, K4, K2tog, (A) K1, SSK, K4. (18 sts) Rows 37-39: Rpt Rows 3-5.
- Row 40: (A) K3, K2tog, K1, (B) SSK, K2, K2tog, (A) K1, SSK, K3. (14 sts) Row 41: (A) P5, (B) P4, (A) P5.
- Row 42: (A) K2, K2tog, K1, (B) SSK, K2tog, (A) K1, SSK, K2. (10 sts) Row 43: (A) P4, (B) P2, (A) P4.
- Cut Yarn B leaving a long tail, and continue in Yarn A.
- Row 44: K1, [K2tog, SSK] twice, K1. (6 sts)
- Row 45: Purl.
- Cut yarn, leaving a long tail. Using a tapestry needle, thread the tail through the stitches left on the needle and pull up tight to gather stitches.

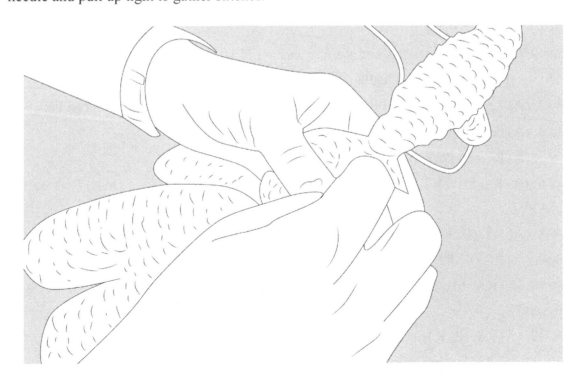

For the Tail:

- Using Yarn B, make a pompom approximately 35mm (13â□„8in) in diameter.

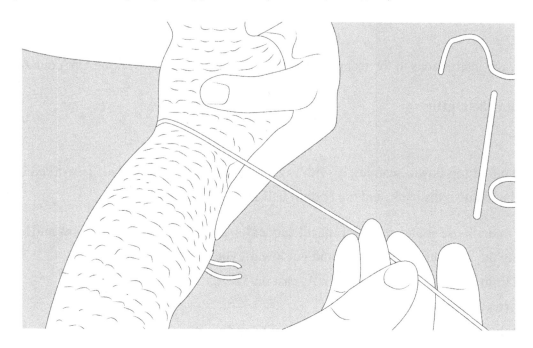

For the Body:

- Work as Standard Body - Plain.

For the Arms (Make 2):

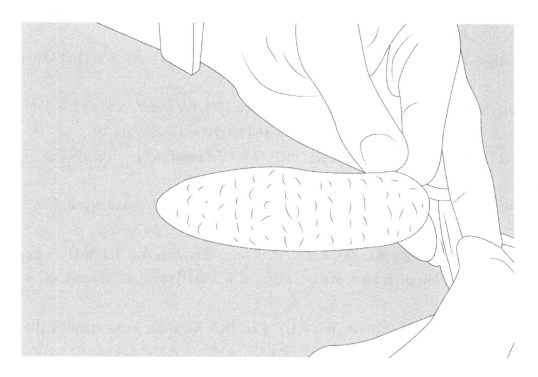

- Work as Standard Arms.

For the Legs (Make 2):

- Work as Standard Legs - Contrast Foot Pad.

Making Up:

- Follow the instructions in the techniques section (see Techniques: Making Up Your Animal).

Instructions for the Outfit:

For the Dress:

The dress is worked top down, seamlessly with raglan cap sleeves. The top half is worked back and forth with a button band down the back, and the bottom half is worked in the round.

- To K1 under loose strand, insert RH needle under loose strand from 2 rows below and knit next stitch, bringing the stitch under the strand and out toward you.
- Using 3mm straight needles and Yarn A, cast on 31 sts.
- Row 1 (ws): Knit.
- Row 2 (buttonhole row): K1, YO, K2tog, knit to end.
- Change to 3.5mm straight needles.
- Row 3: K3, P4, pm, P4, pm, P10, pm, P4, pm, knit to last three sts, K3.
- Row 4: [Knit to marker, m1r, sm, K1, m1l] twice, K2, sl5wyif, [knit to marker, m1r, sm, K1, m1l] twice, knit to end. (39 sts) Row 5: K3, purl to last 3 sts, K3.
- Row 6: [Knit to marker, m1r, sm, K1, m1l] twice, K5, K1 under a loose strand, [knit to marker, m1r, sm, K1, m1l] twice, knit to end. (47 sts) Row 7: As Row 5.
- Row 8: [Knit to marker, m1r, sm, K1, m1l] twice, [K1, sl5wyif] twice, K1, [knit to marker, m1r, sm, K1, m1l] twice, knit to end. (55 sts) Row 9: As Row 5.
- Row 10: [Knit to marker, m1r, sm, K1, m1l] twice, [K4, K1 under loose strand, K1] twice, [knit to marker, m1r, sm, K1, m1l] twice, knit to end. (63 sts) Row 11: As Row 5.
- Row 12: [Knit to marker, m1r, sm, K1, m1l] twice, [sl5wyif, K1] twice, sl5wyif, [knit to marker, m1r, sm, K1, m1l] twice, knit to end. (71 sts) Row 13: As Row 5.
- Row 14: [Knit to marker, m1r, sm, K1, m1l] twice, [K3, K1 under loose strand, K2] 3 times, [knit to marker, m1r, sm, K1, m1l] twice, knit to end. (79 sts) Row 15: As Row 5.
- Row 16 (buttonhole row): K1, YO, K2tog, [knit to marker, m1r, sm, K1, m1l] twice, [sl4wyif, K1, sl1wyif] 3 times, sl3wyif, [knit to marker, m1r, sm, K1, m1l] twice, knit to end. (87 sts) Row 17: As Row 5.
- Row 18: [Knit to marker, m1r, sm, K1, m1l] twice, [K2, K1 under loose strand, K3] 3 times, K2, K1 under a loose strand, [knit to marker, m1r, sm, K1, m1l] twice, knit to end. (95 sts) Row 19: As Row 5.

- Row 20: [Knit to marker, m1r, sm, K1, m1l] twice, [sl3wyif, K1, sl2wyif] 4 times, sl1wyif, [knit to marker, m1r, sm, K1, m1l] twice, knit to end. (103 sts) Row 21: As Row 5.

- Row 22: [Knit to marker, m1r, sm, K1, m1l] twice, [K1, K1 under loose strand, K4] 4 times, K1, K1 under a loose strand, [knit to marker, m1r, sm, K1, m1l] twice, knit to end. (111 sts) Row 23: As Row 5.

- Row 24: [Knit to marker, m1r, sm, K1, m1l] twice, [sl2wyif, K1, sl3wyif] 4 times, sl2wyif, K1, sl2wyif, [knit to marker, m1r, sm, K1, m1l] twice, knit to end. (119 sts) Row 25: K3, purl to marker, remove marker (left back), cast off 25 sts (sleeve), P1, sm; rpt from once more (front and sleeve), purl to last three sts, K3 (right back). (69 sts) Row 26: Knit to marker, sm, K1, m1a, K1, K1 under a loose strand, [K5, K1 under loose strand] 5 times, sm, K1, m1a, knit to end. (71 sts) Row 27: As Row 5.

- Change to 3mm straight needles and Yarn C.

- Row 28: [Knit to marker, m1r, sm, K3, m1l] twice, knit to end. (75 sts) Row 29: Knit.

- Change to 3.5mm straight needles and Yarn A.

- Row 30 (buttonhole row): K1, YO, K2tog, knit to end.

- Row 31: As Row 5.

- Row 32: Knit to marker, m1r, sm, K3, m1l, K13, [K1fb] 6 times, knit to marker, m1r, sm, K3, m1l, knit to end. (85 sts) Row 33: As Row 5.

- Row 34: Knit.

- Row 35: As Row 5.

- Row 36: [Knit to marker, m1r, sm, K3, m1l] twice, knit to end. (89 sts) Rows 37-41: Rpt Rows 33-36 once more, then rpt Row 33 again. (93 sts) Row 42 (buttonhole row): As Row 30.

- Rows 43-44: Rpt Rows 35-36. (97 sts)

- Row 45-51: Rpt Rows 33-36, then rpt Rows 33-35 once more. (101 sts) Rows 52-53: Rpt Rows 34-35.

- Row 54: Transfer sts to a 3.5mm circular needle, [knit to marker, m1r, sm, K3, m1l] twice, knit to last three sts, and slip the last three sts (without working them) onto a cable needle. (105 sts) Join to work in the round:

- Rnd 55: Position cable needle behind first three sts on LH needle, place marker for beginning of a round, knit first st on LH needle together with first st on cable needle, rpt for next two sts, knit to end. (102 sts) Rnd 56-57: Knit 2 rnds.

- Rnd 58: K1, [K1 sl5wyif] to last five sts, K1, sl4wyif.

- Rnd 59: Sl1wyif, knit to end.

- Rnd 60: K4, [K1 under loose strand, K5] to last two sts, K1 under a loose strand, K1.

- Rnd 61: Knit to last st, sl1wyif.

- Rnd 62: Sl4wyif, K1, [sl5wyif, K1] to last st, K1.

- Rnd 63: Knit.

- Rnd 64: K1, [K1 under loose strand, K5] to last five sts, K1 under a loose strand, K4.
- Rnd 65: Knit.
- Rnds 66-80: Rpt Rnds 58-65 once more, then rpt Rnds 58-64 again.
- Change to a 3mm circular needle.
- Rnd 81: Knit.
- Rnd 82: Purl.
- Cast off.

Making Up:

- Block dress.
- Sew buttons in place on the LH button band down the back of the dress, matching them up with the buttonholes.

For the Cardigan:

The cardigan is worked top down, seamlessly, and with a round Fair Isle yoke. The body is worked back and forth in rows, and the sleeves are worked in the round. The button bands (first and last three sts of each row) are worked in Yarn B using the Intarsia method (see Techniques: Colorwork).

- Using Yarn B and 3mm straight needles, cast on 39 sts.
- Row 1 (ws): Knit.
- Row 2 (buttonhole row): K1, YO, K2tog, knit to end.
- Row 3: Knit.
- Change to 3.5mm straight needles.
- Row 4: K4, [K1, K1fb] to last three sts, K3. (55 sts) Row 5: K3, purl to last 3 sts, K3.
- Carrot Chart is worked over the next 14 rows, in stocking stitch and using Fair Isle (Stranded) technique (see Techniques: Colorwork). The chart is repeated across the rows 16 times, and column 1 is worked once more. Read RS rows from right to left and WS rows from left to right. The button bands (first and last three sts of each row) are worked in Yarn B using the Intarsia method (see Techniques: Colorwork).
- Rows 6-9: K3, work Carrot Chart to last three sts, K3. (71 sts) Row 10 (buttonhole row): K1, YO, K2tog, work Carrot Chart to last three sts, K3.
- Rows 11-17: K3, work Carrot Chart to last three sts, K3. (103 sts) Row 18 (buttonhole row): K1, YO, K2tog, work Carrot Chart to last three sts, K3.
- Row 19: K3, work Carrot Chart to last three sts, K3.
- Row 20: (B) K3, (A) [K6, M1] to last four sts, K1, (B) K3. (119 sts) Continue in Yarn B.
- Row 21: K3, purl to last 3 sts, K3.
- Row 22: Knit.

- Row 23: As Row 21.
- Row 24: K18 (left front), without working them, place the next 25 sts onto waste yarn (sleeve), K33 (back), without working them place the next 25 sts onto waste yarn (sleeve), knit to end (right front). (69 sts) Row 25: K3, P16, pm, P33, pm, purl to last three sts, K3.
- Row 26 (buttonhole row): K1, YO, K2tog, [knit to marker, m1r, sm, K2, m1l] twice, knit to end. (73 sts) Row 27: K3, purl to last 3 sts, K3.
- Row 28: Knit.
- Row 29: As Row 27.
- Row 30: [Knit to marker, m1r, sm, K2, m1l] twice, knit to end. (77 sts) Rows 31-33: Rpt Rows 27-29.
- Row 34 (buttonhole row): K1, YO, K2tog, [knit to marker, m1r, sm, K2, m1l] twice, knit to end. (81 sts) Rows 35-40: Rpt Rows 27-30, then rpt Rows 27-28 again. (85 sts) Change to 3mm straight needles.
- Row 41: Knit.
- Row 42 (buttonhole row): K1, YO, K2tog, knit to end.
- Row 43: Knit.
- Cast off.

For the Sleeves:

- Starting under the arm, slip the 25 sts held on waste yarn for one sleeve evenly onto three 3.5mm dpns and rejoin the yarn.
- Using the fourth dpn, start knitting in the round.
- Rnds 1-3: Knit 3 rnds.
- Rnd 4: K1, m1l, knit to last st, m1r, K1. (27 sts) Rnds 5-11: Knit 7 rnds.
- Rnd 12: K1, m1l, knit to last st, m1r, K1. (29 sts) Rnds 13-20: Knit 8 rnds.
- Change to a set of 3mm dpns.
- Rnd 21: Knit.
- Rnd 22: Purl.
- Rnds 23-24: Rpt last two rnds once more.
- Cast off.
- Repeat for the second sleeve.

Making Up:

- Block the cardigan.
- Sew buttons on the front right-hand button band, matching them up with the buttonholes.

CHAPTER 3:
PROBLEMS AND SOLUTIONS

Picking the Incorrect Cast-On

Externally, every cast-on does the same thing by creating loops on a needle that are sweated off by drawing yarn through them with a 2nd needle. However, a standard knitting error made by several beginners can be choosing the incorrect cast-on for a task or altering the cast-on recommended by the pattern developer.

Each type of cast-on has a function beyond developing those first loops. A cast-on sets the phase for the garment. For instance, when casting-on stitches for the leg opening of a sock, the wrong cast-on can make it a fight to obtain the hose on your foot, or worse, it can trigger a fall around your ankles.

Cast-on offers the edge of your job, both stretch and elasticity, and just enough stretch for wearing while supporting the garment's stitching. When you use an elastic cast-on, such as a weaved cast-on, the edge of your project will relocate conveniently. Nonetheless, if you utilize this type of cast-on for something like the neck of a gown that you wish to lie level, it may not support the stitches in the corset, causing it to gap open rather than press flat against your skin.

If a pattern does not state which cast-on to use, numerous knowledgeable knitters use the long-tail cast-on as their go-to. Moderately stretchy with a tip of the framework, the long-tail cast helps many knitters complete their projects.

If the cast-on looks too limited, removing it and beginning again with a different one may be your best option. Believe me. I've done this more frequently than I like to confess, but obtaining the cast-on right makes the rest of the project job far better.

If the builder selected a particular cast-on, but your cast-on side features too much overall flexibility, try casting on with a smaller-sized needle, then proceed to the needle required in the pattern to start your first row. Alternatively, if the cast-on has excessive structure, cast-on with a bigger-sized needle, then move to the appropriate size for the first row.

If the job has too much elasticity at the cast-on edge, usage progresses, and finishing methods add definition to the side.

Binding Off Too Tightly

The tension you use to bind off helps shape your work. Some things happen when stitches are bound off too tightly.

It makes it impossible for you to get precise dimensions, which is generally impossible because a tight bind-off forces your stitches into the project's biggest segment.

Your cast-on for a toe-up sock might be excellent; however, if you bind off too tightly for the leg opening, good luck obtaining that sock over your ankle joint. The same point occurs for neck or wrist openings.

It makes an inflexible straight side that doesn't feel or look good, which frequently contrasts with the soft qualities of the rest of the project.

If you usually knit with tighter tension, switch your stitches to a 1- to 2-dimensional needle that is more important than the one used for the job. Bind off with bigger needles.

Drop it down for the bind-off if you usually maintain tension when knitting by wrapping the working yarn around your fingers. Instead, the working yarn is spread loosely over one finger or between two fingers for stitch catch. Enable the yarn to pass over your fingers or between them to stay clear of the extra tension.

If you knit within the American or United Kingdom style, hold the yarn in the middle of your fingers and cover it freely around the needle to make the bind-off stitch without drawing it as tight as you would for a typical knit or purl sew.

Most importantly, check the tension after the last stitch binding off and before raising the yarn. If it still looks tight, unpick the stitches completely, place them back on the needle, and reshape the bind-off.

Selecting the Wrong Yarn for a Project

Whether knitting from your design or a pattern created by somebody else, choosing the right yarn for the task helps ensure the garment turns out lovely.

Sometimes, you intend to see if a dimension 80 tatting cotton thread knits like the gossamer Shetland. Testing when knitting generates a fun time, so it's definitely a good thing to do. However, choosing the right yarn and understanding how various strands curtain, loss, knit-up, tablet, and more differ has a purpose. In addition, yarn options include yarn weight and color.

When a coat pattern needs a DK weight merino wool, but you choose to use a fingerling weight alpaca, the thickness will not only be off, but the arms, as well as the jacket, will pool at the wrists and the middle part, as the soft fibers of alpaca drape higher than the wool. You may like the appearance, but if not, you may have wasted some effort.

Changing the fiber also impacts the garment. Most pet fibers have a halo, with mohair and angora revealing the most corona. These fuzzy tendrils of texture include extra warmth to a woven garment. The halo hides much of the pattern when selecting them for a shoelace task.

Trying Out Complex Patterns First

Often, people are in a hurry to create the most beautiful, colorful garments without being able to master the stitches or change their yarn colors.

This could result in a disaster which could also be incredibly discouraging. Just keep it simple until you are confident with basic crochet work.

Not Understanding Gauge

Gauge is an aspect of crocheting that is sometimes overlooked because it is not well understood or because individuals just do not want to cope. Suppose you had been crocheting and had entirely neglected to keep track of the gauge - your creations won't fit.

So, what exactly is a gauge, and why do we require it?

The number of stitches, as well as rows you can fit on a 4" × 4" square, is termed a gauge swatch referred to as gauge. Specific stitch numbers are critical for garment size.

Designers would be unable to measure clothes without a gauge swatch, and garments would arrive in various sizes. Even if you're not a designer, you might wonder why you'd need to produce a gauge swatch. Gauge swatches are just as crucial for the crocheter as they are for the designer.

If your gauge isn't the same as what the pattern specifies while sewing a garment or other item, the finished product will be an entirely different size. That means if you're sewing size medium clothing and the swatch has a little more stitches than that of the swatch specifies, your finished product will be smaller in size than the medium size you expected. Your product will be larger than a medium if you use fewer stitches than the gauge asks for.

Weaving in the Ends Incorrectly

You'll see strands of yarn poking out of your craft that you don't want to show up when it's finished. Weaving them in is a good way to remedy them. One of the most challenging aspects of crochet is weaving in ends. It's not that it's difficult; it's simply that it's not enjoyable. However, if the weaving in ends isn't done correctly, it might cause problems.

You don't want to merely cut them off since it will cause your project to unwind too quickly. Instead, leave a long end to weave in as you're trimming. You'll start weaving after threading a yarn needle with a strand of yarn. You'll be threading it all through different threads as you weave in the finish, but don't do it in a straight line. Instead, begin weaving in one way and then switch to the other. This will cause the woven-in to bend, making it more difficult to remove. Whipstitch can also be used to weave the ends in and prevent them from popping out. After you've woven it in as much as possible, snip off the remaining end as near as possible.

Difficulty in Joining Rounds Correctly

When working on a circular project, you often see the term "join the circle." This may be very difficult for beginners because it isn't how you usually go onto the next row while working on a flat design. When a beginner starts knitting, they have no idea how to connect in the round. They always start the round on the wrong stitch and end it on the wrong thread. This messed up the stitch count, which threw the remainder of the design off. But that is something that anyone can be easily remedied.

Let's start by going through how to connect a line of chain stitches to start the project in the round. After you've completed the strand of chain stitches, link the initial chain with a slip stitch at the end of the row to construct your item in the round. When you link the strands of chains, they can get tangled, making the underside of your product appear different than you desire. To avoid this, lay the chain stitches outwards in a circle, as if you're about to connect them, and check to see whether they're twisted. If the strand of chain stitches is twisted, untwist it and connect the strands to form a circle once it looks good.

If you're knitting in the round, you'll connect it if it's not done in continuous rounds. The row (or round) will begin with one or two chains (depending on the stitch) at the first stitch, forming the section you'll connect at the start of the round. It's essentially a stitch marker. After that, knit in each stitch to the finish of the circle. When you come to the end of the circle, be careful not to work a stitch into the chain of 2 stitches. As a result, the round has an excessive number of stitches. Pause at the stitch before the first, and afterward, slip the stitch to the second of the two chains you formed to complete the circle. This completes the round and makes it a complete row. You might need some time to adjust, but you'll acclimate in no time.

Not Understanding the Pattern in Its Entirety

Beginner knitters sometimes leap into a project that appears fun without first reading the instructions, only to discover they have no clue how to complete it. You should always go through a pattern completely before beginning it. You'll be able to determine whether there are any stitches or techniques you'll need to master as you go through the pattern. Frequently, patterns will include instructions in areas beyond a beginner's abilities.

Knitting patterns generally include lessons on attaching garments or components to a project and links to pattern or stitch instructions for unique stitches that some may not be familiar with. You'll be able to see most of these by reading the pattern, ensuring that you won't have to stop knitting midway through to learn a different technique. Even if you wait until later in the pattern to learn it, reading it will alert you there is something new to discover. It might also give you a good idea if you want to create the design now or wait until later.

Worrying About Your Mistakes

Making mistakes is what helps you to learn and improve your work. Lots of practice and even more patience, as well as some creativity, is what makes a successful knitter. You will have to undo your stitches from time to time or even start over again, but that is fine. You are not only learning how to follow instructions; you are also getting used to using your tools and materials, so be patient.

CHAPTER 4:
FAQ

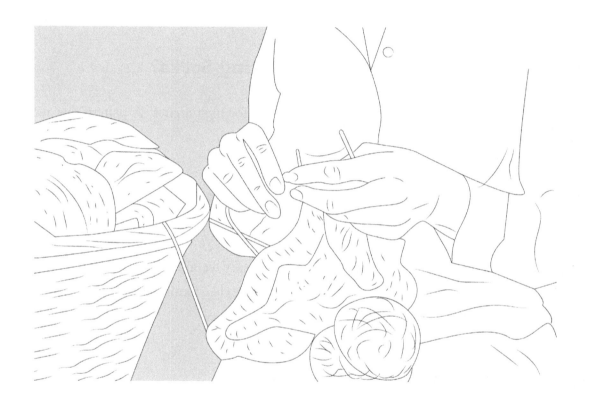

1. What Kind of Yarn Do I Use for Knitting Socks?

Most knitters recommend a medium-weight yarn for knitting socks as it's easier to work with and gives a highly comfortable finish. Of course, as you experiment with varying patterns, you'll develop your preferences.

2. How to Knit Socks on Two Straight Needles?

Many sock patterns – particularly those aimed at beginners – work from straight needles. You will have been able to practice a few of these while working through this book. If you're looking for more, this is a great resource.

3. How Do You Knit Socks on Four Needles?

This guide will also see patterns working on four double-pointed needles. Try this resource if it's a technique you've enjoyed and want to work on more.

4. What's an Easy Pattern for Knitting Socks?

You have covered many patterns aimed specifically at knitting beginners for socks, but you can find a lot more here.

5. How Do You Get High Arches in Knitting Socks?

A sock with a heel flap and gusset is more accommodating for high arches. A pattern that works for this theory can be found here.

6. Is it Easier to Knit Socks with a Sock Loom Than Knitting Needles?

Different people prefer different techniques for knitting. Now that you're familiar with hand knitting using this book, it is likely that you'll prefer to work all of the necessary techniques by hand – but there is no harm in trying a loom! Many prefer the relaxation and methodical style of knitting that comes with doing it by hand – plus the level of satisfaction at a completed project.

7. Should You Knit a Swatch Gauge?

It's always advisable, especially for beginners, to knit a swatch gauge to ensure that you have chosen the correct yarn and needles for a pattern. Failing to do so can result in the finished project being the wrong size, and no one wants to waste time on that!

8. Why is Knitting a Good Skill to Have?

Knitting is a brilliant skill that can help you create various products – everything from toys to clothing. But not only that, it's scientifically proven to improve your mood, mind, and body. It's a therapeutic skill that you will not regret learning!

9. Does It Cost a Lot to Knit?

Knitting can be done very cheaply if you know the right places to look. Local haberdashery stores will sell a wide range of products from high quality to budget, so it is a skill that applies to everyone.

10. What is Knitting in Tandem?

Tandem knitting is a technique for knitting socks, gloves, or anything in the round that comes in pairs and uses 9 DPNs. It casts on for both items in the pair simultaneously and involves completing a portion of one of the pair, then the same portion of the other item of the pair.

11. Is Crocheting Harder Than Knitting?

Crocheting differs from knitting because it uses one hook rather than two needles. Different people prefer other skills, so practicing both is the best way to determine which one you find easier and more suitable.

12. Where Can I Find Some Great Knitting Patterns?

Knitting patterns can be found in haberdashery stores, but they are also available online. Type 'Knitting Patterns' into any search engine, and you will be spoilt for choice.

CONCLUSION

Thank you for reading this book. You learned how to knit using simple steps in this book. These clear instructions will assist you in mastering the skill, especially if you are a beginner. Knitting is a fascinating hobby with endless possibilities. After you've mastered the fundamentals, begin with simple projects that take little time to complete and are less prone to errors. A few projects may take you longer to complete than others, but don't worry. That simply means you will learn more as you go.

Knitting is distinct from other art forms, and people frequently wonder about the origins of knitted items and knitting itself. Knitting has been practiced for thousands of years. Knitting was initially used to create textiles for clothing.

It is always preferable to begin with the fundamentals to become comfortable with everything you do or learn. This book has taught you important aspects of knitting that will help you succeed and allow you to develop your style by making knitting designs. It will assist you in determining where to begin with your knitting project in terms of difficulty.

It is best to start with a small knitting project if you are new to knitting. You can even choose a job that requires you to master the fundamentals before attempting more complex models. It may be tempting to choose more innovative designs, but if you focus on them, you may become frustrated.

With these simple and easy patterns, you're practicing everything you need to know to move on to more complex patterns for perfect gifts and a relaxing afternoon. This book will be your ultimate knitting resource, covering everything you need to know. It includes tried-and-true instructions for knitting the best way possible.

Knitting is distinct from other art forms, and people frequently wonder about the origins of knitted items and knitting itself. Knitting has been practiced for thousands of years. Knitting was initially used to create textiles for clothing.

This book will teach you all the things you need to know about knitting, regardless of your level of experience. It will walk you through your journey to learn everything there is to know about knitting, from the most basic ideas to the most complex ones. After reading this book, you should be well on becoming an accomplished knitter. This book has taught you the fundamentals of knitting. You'll master these skills through trial and error as you practice, and you'll be ready to learn more advanced knitting techniques in no time - plus, you'll have cuddly knitted creations to show for your efforts. Welcome to the global knitting community!

Knitting is no longer necessary; however, it has a large following of people who enjoy the craft as a hobby. Why should they not? Knitters benefit from physical and psychological health benefits and the apparent use of creating useful and unique articles and garments.

You're probably one of those people looking for the best source of information on how to knit properly, and you've come to the right place. This book will definitely help you discover your knitting abilities!

I hope this book is of great assistance to you. Thank you, and good luck.